MW00487439

To my awesome wife Erica and the best kids in the world, Cassidy and Alexander (AJ)

CONTENTS

Chapter		Page
	Genesis	6
	Prologue	7
	Introduction	9
1	Chaos	10
2	History	18
3	Third Parties	31
4	Tea Time	37
5	Disruptive Causation	44
6	The Path to Chaos	67
7	The Tribes	84
8	The Presidential Campaigns	92
9	Republican National Committee	107
10	Recent National Convention History	119
11	2016 Republican National Convention	130
12	Rules	138
13	Contests	145
14	Delegates	147
15	State Order and Distribution	150
16	SINOs	154
17	Delegation Selection	156
18	National Convention Ballots	199
19	Key Players	201
20	Prisoners Dilemma	206
21	Vice Presidential Selection	207
22	Established No Longer	210
23	Total Chaos	211
24	Cost of Chaos	214
25	Potential Solutions	216
26	Conclusion	217
	About the Author	221
Appendix A	Top Things You Can Do	223

REALTIMEBOOKS

This book is a product of RealTimeBooks, a book publishing company that is pioneering the concept of books that are highly sensitive to a specific moment in time.

There are plenty of books that cover elections and political movements from a historical perspective of years, decades, or even a century later.

Conversely, there are plenty of magazines and news sites that write extended news pieces about campaigns in an election year, and news sites that write real-time day to day news.

RealTimeBooks focuses on publishing books written by known authors who have time-sensitive knowledge that might interest the public.

This (unedited) version of the book was written and printed prior to the February 20th, 2016 South Carolina Primary.

ACKNOWLEDGEMENTS

My wife and children, for putting up with me.

My Dad, Chuck Yob, for teaching me the importance of loyalty, friendship, and not turning opponents into enemies. I didn't always listen. :)

Terri Lynn Land, for giving me my first chance for a statewide victory in the Michigan Secretary of State race.

John Weaver and Mike Dennehy, for giving me my first big opportunity in politics.

Sarah Palin, Rand Paul, Ted Cruz, Rick Santelli, and millions of concerned Americans across the country who were concerned for our children and grandchildren's future and started an organic movement to change the country.

Curt Clawson and Ben Sasse-- who are representative of a new type of outsider-- both highly credible conservatives, yet also electable in a general election. We need more candidates like them.

Ambassador Ron Weiser, for facilitating communication with the other side of the party.

Rick Snyder, Brian Calley, and Bill Schuette for sticking with me after we won.

And most importantly, to the establishment for always overreacting and making all of this possible.

GENESIS

The writing for this book began in 2010. The initial working title of it was *Path to the North Star*. It was a "how to" manual describing how to nominate a Tea Party-backed candidate for President in 2012. It was a thought experiment focused on the idea that a candidate like Sarah Palin could become the presidential nominee by winning state convention contests across the country rather than through the traditional primary process. This is now nearly impossible because of recent rules changes as described later in this book.

The initial plan began with a bottom-up strategy of winning local party precinct, county, and district races in states across the country through a combination of Tea Party and liberty supporters that would team up to take on longtime establishment Republicans.

The tactics manifested in the election of several "outsider" candidates across the country in 2010, 2012, and 2014 including Michigan Governor Rick Snyder, Michigan Lt Governor Brian Calley, Michigan Attorney General Bill Schuette, Michigan Congressman John Moolenaar, Florida Congressman Curt Clawson, and Nebraska US Senator Ben Sasse, among others.

The rules for the Republican National Convention were changed dramatically after the 2012 election in an effort to prevent a conservative underdog from contesting the convention against an establishment-backed presumptive nominee.

The book has morphed significantly over the years prior to being released in 2016 through RealTimeBooks.

PROLOGUE

Curly Haugland is the longtime Republican National Committeeman from North Dakota who is viewed as an anti-establishment rules expert on the Republican National Committee (RNC).

He has long argued that the Chairman of the Republican National Committee should be a member of the RNC. He has been successful in creating a movement within the membership to elect one of their own as Chairman rather than someone from outside the committee.

He also fought for rules that make it easier for the national convention to nominate the presidential nominee from a contested convention made up of conservative, independent-minded delegates rather than a primary process that culminates in rubber stamping the presumptive nominee at a national convention.

He argues that in fact delegates to the national convention are not bound as a result oft he RNC rules that were passed in recent years, and believes any binding is subject to challenge and ultimate revision in the convention rules committee or on the floor of the convention.

Haugland's expertise is particularly relevant because he is a longtime member of the national committee and an important player in the North Dakota delegate process.

North Dakota is electing delegates to the National Convention who will not be bound because they do not have a preference poll and therefore are free agents at the convention.

Haugland strongly believes Cleveland will be a contested convention.

PROLOGUE

By Republican National Committeeman Curly Haugland

Chaos may be an understatement in describing the 2016 Republican National Convention.

The first indication of rough weather for the Republican Party in 2016 was at the convention in 2012. Thanks to the party's customary practice of declaring a "presumptive nominee" in advance of the actual convention nomination, the campaign was allowed control of the entire convention; but, it was the mischief in the Convention Rules Committee that began the perfect political storm.

To keep Ron Paul from being nominated and to preclude a challenge to the Romney re-election in 2016, attorney Ben Ginsberg authored an amendment to Rule 40(b) that requires candidates to demonstrate the support of a majority of the permanently seated delegates from eight states prior to having their name placed in nomination at the convention.

That provision alone is, at best, a tropical depression. Add an open race with a large field of well qualified candidates and the storm intensifies. Add a self-funding billionaire to the candidate mix and a general mood of unrest among the electorate and you have a political hurricane.

Now in uncharted territory, the party will soon be faced with the added challenges of managing a convention, the rules for which are widely misunderstood due to lack of use for many recent conventions.

For instance, some people in the Republican Party are convinced that delegates to the convention are "bound" or forced to cast their votes according to the results of primary or caucus events; thus transferring the right to choose the nominee from the delegates to the convention to the voters in primaries and caucuses.

This will all be sorted out by the delegates assembled in July when we meet as the Republican National Convention of 2016.

The only thing that is certain is that there will be chaos in Cleveland.

INTRODUCTION

DREAMS OF FLOOR FIGHTS DANCING IN OUR HEADS

Many political operatives have long-held fantasies about a brokered Republican National Convention that throws the nomination contest into chaos and gives tremendous authority to grassroots activists rather than establishment party leaders and billionaire bundlers.

But dreams of floor fights rarely come true.

The last time a Republican National Convention was truly contested was in 1976 when former Governor Ronald Reagan and President Gerald R. Ford fought for the right to take on Governor Jimmy Carter.

The last time the convention required multiple ballots was in 1948 when New York Governor Thomas Dewey defeated several other candidates including Senator Robert Taft of Ohio, Governor Harold Stassen of Minnesota, Governor Earl Warren of California, and Senator Arthur Vandenberg of Michigan.

This book is based on the premise that the 2016 Republican National Convention in Cleveland will be the first truly contested Republican National Convention in 40 years, and the first convention that will require multiple ballot in 68 years.

History will be made once again as result of changes in the way campaigns are run, momentum for outsider candidates, changing technology that impacts campaigns, rule changes by the RNC, and the most wide-open presidential race in a generation.

The results of Iowa and New Hampshire have made clear that our wildest political fantasies will come true on the banks of the Cuyahoga.

1. CHAOS

Come July, thousands of politicians, party elders, campaign consultants, activists, and reporters will descend on Cleveland for a suspenseful, dramatic, and chaotic Republican National Convention.

As a rule, conventions are not supposed to be dramatic; they're carefully choreographed by the presidential nominee and his or her political team to have said exactly what they believe should be said to set the stage for the general election. That's not going to happen in 2016. All those activists and politicos won't be attending the same old dog and pony show that they can usually expect at a convention. Instead, they will arrive spoiling for a fight - a fight to pick the Republican nominee for president, and maybe a fight for the future of the GOP itself.

This fight has been brewing for almost a decade. The nationwide conservative political groundswell that began in 2009 and developed into the Tea Party waves of 2010 and 2014 is now buoying several outsider candidates. The success of the outsiders, combined with the establishment's attempts to keep their grip on control of the party, will culminate in a messy, chaotic, contested Republican National Convention. The fight holds danger and opportunity for everyone involved. It could fragment the Republican Party for a generation, lead to the creation of a new third party, or it could lay the foundation for a new winning conservative coalition. Either way, the chaos in Cleveland will set the course for the GOP and the conservative movement at a critical time. None of the outcomes are certain.

To get ready for the first brokered convention in decades, conservatives need to know two things; first, who are the power players, and second, could this really happen?

You've heard of Jeb Bush, Ted Cruz, and Donald Trump, but what about Amata Radewagen, Curly Haugland, and Governor Eddie Baza Calvo of Guam? Who are these folks? Why do they matter? An army of political professionals, anonymous to the broader public but influential within a convention fight could play a decisive role in picking the candidate who will face Hillary Clinton in the general election. That doesn't have to be as bad as it sounds. In modern politics, conventions provide grassroots conservatives with a chance to counteract the political establishment. Remember, Mike Lee was the first Tea Party candidate to win a U.S. Senate seat and he pulled it off by knocking out an incumbent establishment Republican at the Utah State Party Convention. That can only happen in Cleveland if conservatives learn the rules, study up on the process, and make sure the people who actually have the power to vote for the nominee — the delegates to the convention — come from the ranks of conservatives and vote for conservative principles.

Could this really happen?

Most of the political establishment thinks everything you read in this vein is a bunch of nonsense. They assume that because something has not happened in a long time, it won't happen in the future. That might be a good rule of thumb, but it's no guarantee. If the conventional wisdom of reporters came to pass, Hillary Clinton wouldn't have lost to Barack Obama in 2008. The Tea Party wouldn't exist. Mike Lee, Rand Paul, Pat Toomey, Marco Rubio, Ted Cruz, and Ben Sasse wouldn't be United States Senators. Bernie Sanders wouldn't be giving Hillary Clinton all she can handle in early primary states. Donald Trump sure as hell would not be the frontrunner in the Republican primary.

In fairness to the pundits, there are plenty of good reasons why brokered conventions don't happen anymore. As *The Washington Examiner*'s Michael Barone pointed out in December, such conventions are kind of a relic of the 19th century, before the invention of cell phones and the internet, when party leaders had to meet in person to hash out the biggest political fights. The increasing importance of primary elections and various rules changes has meant that most delegates are awarded before the convention, especially given that the winner of the early states tends to get the most media coverage, raise the most money, and ultimately sweep the last states that vote. That's why Republicans have had a "presumptive nominee" well before the start of every convention since the 1976 presidential election.

Political elites who believe contested conventions have gone the way of the dinosaur can argue that the 1976 race is the exception that proves the rule. It's unthinkable in these days that a sitting president would face a primary challenge, but President Gerald Ford was a unique incumbent. The former House minority leader had never won a race outside of his congressional district, so he commanded far less loyalty in his party than most men in his position. He had the job because Richard Nixon appointed him in 1973 to replace Vice President Spiro Agnew, who had resigned in the face of bribery charges. When Nixon resigned several months later over the Watergate scandal, Ford moved into the Oval Office as the heir to a challenging administration. On the other side of the ledger was California Governor Ronald Reagan, a conservative hero and the most talented American politician since Jack Kennedy. When the candidates arrived in Kansas City, Missouri for the convention, neither man had enough delegates to win the nomination, but Ford convinced enough delegates to come his way to clinch the race on the first ballot.

There are no perfect analogies in history, but in some ways, the 1976 race suggests why a contested convention is so much more likely to happen this year than in previous elections. The GOP establishment is weaker than it has been in decades. Nixon's political machine hurt Ford as much as it helped. Initial frontrunner Jeb Bush was weighed down by his last name. The '76 primary season also shows the importance of the primary calendar and the rules about how the elections affect the delegates to the convention. Ford won the first six states that voted, starting with Iowa and New Hampshire. Reagan was on the verge of dropping out. Fortunately for Reagan, the seventh state to go to the polls was the conservative stronghold of North Carolina. Senator Jesse Helms, the conservative firebrand, pulled out all the stops and Reagan lived to fight another day. A similar thing could happen this cycle with a candidate winning big in the conservative states that vote on March 1 such as Texas. Speaking of Texas, the 10th state to hold a primary in 1976 was the first one to require that its convention delegates vote for the winner of the primary. At that point, it didn't matter that Ford had won eight states and Reagan had won just two — Reagan was the only guy in the race who had delegates who by rule *had* to vote for him at the convention. That meant he was in the race for the long haul.

You know who else didn't drop out? Ford, of course -- and this leads to one of the most important general principles we can extract from 1976 and apply to the 2016 race: when outsider candidates struggle to get traction, establishment politicians and donors pressure them to drop out for the good of the party; when the establishment struggles, they don't give up. If Donald Trump or Ted Cruz win a bunch of early states, there's no way the party greybeards will tell their favorites to quit and make way for the nominee. They will fight tooth and nail all summer long. Even in its weakened state, the establishment is still powerful. Ford *did* ultimately win after all- and that's why they never give up.

Not all victories are created equal, however. It's the great irony of the 2016 primary season that the establishment may struggle to take control of the election precisely because of one of their most recent victories over the outsiders. In 2012, Mitt Romney's team saw Ron Paul as a problem and they used their power at the Republican National Convention to weaken him. They started by changing the rules to require the delegates at the convention to vote for whichever candidate won their home state's primary or caucus. The new rule stripped Paul of the delegates who were planning to vote for him since he had not won their state primary. That's not all. Romney's team also changed the rules about who could be considered a candidate for the nomination at the convention. Under the old rules, any candidate who won "a plurality of the delegates from each of five (5) or more states" could be considered for the nomination. Romney's team rewrote the rules to require candidates to win "a majority of the delegates from each of eight (8) or more states" in order for a candidate's name to be placed into nomination on the first ballot. Another win for the establishment, or so it seemed.

Fast forward four years and those rule changes look like a disaster in the making for anyone who had hoped to stop an outsider running for the presidential nomination. With so many strong candidates in the field this year, the establishment favorite may have a hard time winning a majority of delegates in eight states. More likely, multiple candidates will win several states. Regardless of who wins the plurality, there are few winner-take-all states so ballot access will be difficult for anyone. That doesn't happen in most years because the primary season is stretched out and weaker candidates run out of money. This year is different.

Because of super PACs, it only takes a single billionaire to keep a losing candidate in the race (that's how Newt Gingrich survived for so long in 2012). The campaign calendar will also tempt candidates who might have dropped out in previous years to keep competing. A majority of states and territories will vote in March, so a candidate who loses early won't have to wait more than a week for another chance to right the ship. Because the RNC decided that states voting before March 15 must award their delegates proportionally, whereas states voting after March 15 could be winner-take-all, a losing candidate could get a big boost by winning later in the month. Ironically, the RNC hoped that schedule would shorten the campaign cycle, when in fact the new process will lengthen the race and ensure that also-rans get a chance to win a significant number of delegates.

If only someone could have warned them that central planning never works.

Under the old convention rules, the establishment used to be able to try and convince delegates to vote for someone other than the candidate their state had backed. ("Yes, McCain won your state, but Bush is the nominee, so how about we all come together here at our state convention for the sake of unity now?") That's not possible any more. If the primary process concludes and no one has won the nomination outright, the delegates are frozen in place - most will likely be bound to vote in accordance with the delegate allocation rules and the results of their primary or caucus. Even those rules aren't clear.

In other words, the rule change that benefitted the Romney team in 2012 will now make it impossible for the establishment to eke out a win on the first ballot the way Ford did in 1976. Instead, it will be time to buckle up for a good old fashioned convention floor fight.

That fight will begin well before the convention starts and, once again, the Romney team's rule changes will influence the outcome. For example, what if Marco Rubio were to win a majority of delegates in, say, only seven states? He'd be one state short of the eight victories required to compete in Cleveland. Fortunately for him, there are three states and three territories that don't hold a primary or caucus, so they can back any candidate at the convention. Guam is one of those six, so Rubio might try to win the endorsement of Governor Eddie Baza Calvo away from Senator Ted Cruz who Governor Calvo initially endorsed. If Rubio succeeds, he could be on a path to winning the convention fight. If he fails (since other campaigns will try to box him out), his candidacy is over unless he can change the rules. And that's the point- Eddie Baza Calvo is likely a guy you have never heard of, but he could have a huge impact on the outcome of the convention.

If the first ballot vote at the convention is a formality, the second ballot will be a free-for-all because delegates will be free to vote for anyone they like. The fundamental question is, "How will conservative and libertarian activists ultimately cast their votes at the convention?" There are limits to the power of political elites to influence the outcome of a contested convention and delegates are the ones who have the final say over who wins the nomination. In most places, the establishment does not choose the delegates. Instead, the delegates are elected at county and state Republican Party conventions by conservatives. That could spell disaster for candidates like Jeb Bush who might walk into the convention feeling optimistic, only to find out that many of his delegates are actually conservative activists who plan to vote for someone else when given the opportunity- supporters in name only. Donald Trump could win the Michigan primary, but if he doesn't bother to have his supporters win the local battles that decide who gets to vote at the national convention, he could see half his delegates go to Cruz on a later ballot. Or his own delegates could work against him on the convention committees. Ron Paul won many of his delegates by beating Mitt Romney's team at local conventions in 2012. Well-organized outsider candidates such as Ted Cruz could run the same play this year.

Given the potential for the convention to open without a preordained nominee, there is even the possibility for an outside candidate- one who didn't even run a campaign or announce his candidacy- to emerge victorious from the convention.

It is not unusual for some high-level Republicans (and of course grassroots conservatives) to be unhappy with their choice of candidates. The 2008 election included a sustained, yet relatively quiet effort, to convince Haley Barbour to join the race for president. The 2012 election included a less quiet and very aggressive effort to convince Mitch Daniels to run for president and later an effort to convince Chris Christie.

The 2016 election seemingly includes something for everyone. There are 15 different flavors of ice cream to choose from from along the ideological and establishment spectrums and the candidates who drop out of the race as the convention approaches will have strong supporters who invested time, money, blood, sweat, and tears over the last two years to help them get elected. Those people will be unhappy with the remaining choices because they spent time bashing those candidates on social media, fighting with those candidates' supporters, and convincing friends and family that their choice was the only choice. Many will still harbor negative feelings.

It will make matters worse that rather than endorse another candidate, most candidates who exit the race will do so by suspending their campaigns and never officially "drop out."

This will increase the chaos of the convention, but more importantly it will increase the unpredictable nature of ballot access and the later ballots of the convention.

These factors could result in party leaders and operatives coming to someone like Mitt Romney or Paul Ryan and asking him to allow his name to be put into nomination at the Republican National Convention. We may at some point hear "the Javelin has landed".

But there will also be those who understand that the delegates are mostly very conservative, and would see the need for a candidate who could unite both wings of the party- someone who the establishment both trusts to win a general election and is a conservative outsider that the grassroots know and trust. Senators Mike Lee, Tim Scott, and Ben Sasse come to mind as leaders who could win a convention fight.

In truth, there's really no way to predict how a contested convention will unfold- and reporters will have a hard time explaining it in real-time because most of them have never covered one before and don't know the rules and procedures. Hopefully, this book will give grassroots activists the background information they need to understand what they're watching when the convention finally begins. You can get to know the tribes of campaign operatives and party bureaucrats, the friends and enemies who will be making deals at the convention. You can also learn which states or territories could be the bellwethers of the convention and why they could play that role. And if it inspires some of you to become delegates yourselves, all the better. You'll have a front row seat for the most interesting Republican National Convention of your lifetime.

2. HISTORY

There is a long history of presidential nominations being decided at contested or brokered conventions. In some cases, there would be several candidates running, and powerful party leaders from each state would get together at the convention and negotiate the votes from their state in smoke-filled back rooms far from the glare of television cameras.

This continued up until the TV era when the political parties seemed to figure out that voters at home didn't like the proverbial sausage-making that occurred at these conventions, and that these activities ultimately dissuaded voters from supporting the candidates involved.

There are a few contested conventions that are worth examining in order to fully understand their history and to understand what that might mean for the chaos that will occur in Cleveland.

Convention of 1860

The election of 1860 was historic for any number of reasons. It was only the second Republican Party convention – the Whig party had recently gone under. It was the first held for a mass audience – Chicago, then a city of barely 100,000 people, ponied up thousands of dollars to build a temporary structure to host the event. In a building known as "the wigwam," they constructed the largest convention hall in the country at the time, holding 10,000 people. It was designed brilliantly, so that, pre-electricity, a speaker could be heard throughout.

There were few primaries at the time, and candidates often didn't participate in them. It was simply a matter of getting delegates at the state level and/or winning them at the convention.

Though the run up to the convention would look unfamiliar to modern political operatives, the convention itself would look very familiar to any of us who have done state and local conventions.

William H. Seward was the leading candidate for the nomination. He was from New York and had the money people and media expecting his victory. A leading opponent was Abraham Lincoln, Kentucky born, but a native son to Illinois where the convention was being held. Pennsylvania, Ohio and Missouri also had favorite son candidates, making this a multiple ballot, multiple candidate field.

In this race, as in the race we will see later in 1948, with a well-funded, establishment, New York frontrunner and a conservative, Midwestern upstart, the dynamics of momentum and collusion between lower tier candidates made all the difference.

Seward concentrated on getting as big a first ballot lead as possible. This made sense because his New York delegation controlled 70 of the 233 votes needed for the nomination. He concentrated on adding to that coalition to win outright, but in doing so, ignored the favorite son candidates and their votes for too long.

Lincoln has been universally acknowledged as a great president, but what is not as widely known about him is that he was a master political tactician - the best of his era for sure. He devised what was known as the Lincoln Four Step for ensuring victory in an election by systematically identifying and securing supporters in an election, something that set in motion the modern precinct and grassroots-driven campaigns that are still widely seen today.

In 1860, Lincoln meticulously strategized for the convention- even taking into account momentum and floor strength. Lincoln appointed his trusted friend David Davis to be his "delegate hunter" and let him loose with broad power but strict instructions.

It should be noted that at the time, it was considered bad form for the candidates to actually attend the conventions. Neither Lincoln nor Seward would be in Chicago for the actual event. But Seward, recognizing Lincoln's hometown advantage with the crowd, sent railroad cars full of supporters to Illinois.

Lincoln's team deviously made counterfeit tickets and instructed their people to arrive early, so that when Seward's trains arrived from New York, they could not get in.

More importantly, Lincoln always knew he could not win on a first ballot, so he planned for the second and third ballots as part of his overall strategy. He directed his team to work the delegations of the favorite sons and other groups of delegates very hard with the goal of being the second highest vote-getter on the first ballot, but gaining on each subsequent one.

The plan worked. Lincoln denied Seward a first ballot win and came in second. He gained on the second ballot and the third, then won outright.

With each ballot, more delegates saw Lincoln as the one gaining. They saw a frontrunner denied a victory and an upstart closing in on him. They saw Seward as having a ceiling, and Lincoln as the coalition-builder with the anti-Seward forces.

These are important dynamics in a convention. Entire blocs of votes can be swayed by momentum- perceived or real- and by impressions that a candidate is maxed out or potentially growing. Everyone wants to win.

Convention of 1948: The First Modern Convention
The convention of 1948 is notable for several reasons. First, it took three ballots for the Republican nominee to be decided. Second, it featured the first presidential debate on radio. Third, it showed the differences in campaign strategy- again between an establishment led, party-driven campaign and a conservative ideological insurgency.

The campaign of 1948 actually began several years earlier. We think of that as a modern problem – journalists wring their hands every few years about how campaigns begin earlier and earlier every cycle, but like many things told to you by journalists who do not study history, it is largely untrue. Declared candidacies may start earlier, but the real campaign has always begun in earnest sometimes years earlier.

In this case, it began with Harry Truman's assumption of the presidency upon the death of Franklin Roosevelt in 1945. Roosevelt had defeated New York Governor Thomas Dewey in his last election by 20 states, 3.6 million votes, and 200 electoral votes. The margin wasn't all that close. Dewey, a popular, moderate New York governor, ran as an opponent of the New Deal, but never gained traction against a three term, wartime president credited by many voters as responsible for relieving the ills of the Great Depression and defending the country against Germany and Japan.

Truman was another matter. A failed haberdasher with the look and speaking ability more normally associated with a backroom office worker than a president, the 1945-46 version of Truman, especially in public perception, bears little resemblance to the Truman of the history books today. He was considered an accidental president whose chances for re-election were very weak, and was in danger of not even being re-nominated by his own party.

Against this backdrop was a civil war within the Republican Party, with one side being led by Governor and former nominee Thomas Dewey, and the other by conservative hero Robert Taft of Ohio. Taft was a senator who vocally opposed the New Deal, and was a leader in the fight against labor unions and American intervention overseas.[1]

Taft also led the Republican counterattack against the largely unchecked power of labor unions. Since the 1935 passage of the Wagner Act, which greatly expanded union power, conservatives had begun fighting (mostly at the state level) for curbs on this power. Movements were active across America for what became known as "right to work"- freedom from having to

---

[1] Non-intervention in foreign affairs was considered the more conservative position, back in the time before the neoconservative takeover of Republican foreign policy. It was Dewey the liberal and his allies, mostly northeastern elites, who pushed for a larger American role in the world, more military intervention, and a stronger sense of obligation to right wrongs in international affairs.

pay union bosses for the privilege of getting or keeping a job. Taft led this fight in the Senate, with the bill allowing for state Right to Work laws bearing his name.

Many saw 1946-1948 as an ideological battle between the liberal/progressive Republicans and the conservatives – and to some extent it was. The direction of the party was impacted by many things that happened in those years, including things that happened at the Democratic convention that year.

But the 1948 election didn't end up being swayed by ideology. It was swayed by good old fashioned party politics and bosses - never a good sign for the conservatives.

The battle began in the 1946 midterms with a battle for control of the national party. The Taft conservative forces saw an opportunity, and mounted their first real challenge to the national party establishment, prevailing with their own man, Carroll Reece of Tennessee after three ballots. Reece and Taft sought to change the policies and direction of the RNC, but found that it wasn't that simple, with state party chairs, committeemen, and others entrenched in positions that wouldn't easily be moved until after the next presidential elections.

In the midterms, the party's election focus paid dividends with conservatives being added to the ranks of national and state elected officials, with credit given to Taft and his allies for both their election work and their bolder legislative strategy in Congress.

Taft entered into the 1948 election cycle perceived – especially in his own mind – as the national frontrunner for the nomination, and therefore the presidency, with Truman being perceived as a weak candidate.

Dewey wasn't even necessarily seen as the main challenger to Taft's nominative victory. Minnesota liberal Harold Stassen, a fresh face who more clearly embodied the progressive Republican ideology, was seen as his main competition.

But Dewey had several advantages; he had run twice before, losing the nomination once and winning it the second time, he had won multiple elections in a large, wealthy state, he had an experienced and often cutthroat campaign staff and organization, and he had absolutely no hesitation about using all of these advantages to raise money, bribe delegations, strike deals, wine, dine, and entertain potential allies, and put himself in a much better position than anyone thought possible going into the convention.

During the primaries, Taft won more than double the votes than Dewey, yet Dewey entered Philadelphia in June 1948 with more delegates on his side - though not enough for a majority.

The Philadelphia convention was unusual because both parties were holding their convention in the same city several weeks apart. Both were going through major ideological battles - liberal vs. conservative, region vs. region- and wrestled with some of the same issues- communism and foreign affairs, civil rights, and how to move forward after the New Deal. How the parties dealt with these issues had major implications going forward, though that was not evident during primary season.

In the sweltering heat of Philadelphia that year, and in full view of the first convention television audiences, both parties bared their ideological and organizational divides for the world to see.

The convention hall did not have air conditioning, and it was one of the hottest summers in Philadelphia history. With nearly 12,000 people packed into the arena, as well as the newly arrived television lights and equipment, it was brutal. Hundreds of people had to be treated for heat-related issues. Open doors led to pigeons attacking delegates on the floor.

A divided party, suffocating heat, and shit literally flying everywhere. (Those of you who have attended conventions will recognize that the invention of air conditioning has not changed the other two staples of most conventions.)

Dewey's campaign team was led by Herbert Brownell, the former RNC Chairman and his Dewey's campaign manager from the past cycle. Brownell devised the strategy that led Dewey to focus on delegates rather than primaries, on party officials rather than rank and file, on disguising views rather than fighting ideological battles, and in wooing hundreds of delegates.

Brownell's location in New York City made for prime entertainment - he lavished delegates with meals, tickets to sporting events, sightseeing - you name it. Dewey's campaign also concentrated heavily on raising money. As governor of the large, wealthy state of New York, they succeeded quickly. No expense was spared.

They also devised a strategy of picking off parts of delegations they knew they could not win outright. While Taft focused his efforts on a regional strategy, trying to fully lock up the states where he was strongest, Dewey aimed to split delegations where he was weaker - a tactic that worked well.

A good example was Alabama. Taft was stronger throughout the south, and Alabama was no exception. Dewey met with the top two party officials, and saw that the top official was ideologically predisposed to Taft, so he focused his efforts on the second in command. The Republican Party of Alabama existed largely to dispense patronage in the state – there were few elected officials and little chance of carrying the state back then if you were a Republican (quite a difference from today).

With promises of patronage and positions in a Dewey administration, Brownell was able to pick off the second in command as well as roughly one third of the delegates. Repeated in other states, Dewey ended up with many more delegates than anyone believed possible, especially once state delegations were released after the first ballot.

Taft was thwarted by something else that will be familiar to those who have followed modern elections, particularly the election of 2016 – a plethora of candidates. Fifteen candidates – among them the Speaker of the House, senators, congressmen, governors – all vied for the nomination.

In something that will not be familiar to modern students of campaigns, many of them didn't run national campaigns. They ran as "favorite son" candidates, locking their delegates from their state in order to deny any one candidate a majority, and then holding them back for deal-making.

Senator Edward Martin from Pennsylvania was one such candidate. Martin was a Republican institution in Pennsylvania, having served as state party chair, governor and now senator. He controlled the 73 electoral votes, and did not hold them hostage to ideology, or a particular position, but rather for the best promise of the spoils of victory. Dewey's team was able to convince him that those better came from them, and Pennsylvania lined up for Dewey right before the convention began in their state.

Others in nomination from the floor included the longtime Governor of California Earl Warren and war hero General Douglas MacArthur.

There was no lack of talent, intrigue, or pageantry at his convention - Taft paraded around a live elephant at one point.

On the first ballot, Dewey shocked Taft by getting 434 of the 1094 votes to Taft's 224, with Stassen trailing at 157 and others splitting the rest.

The forces against Dewey tried in vain to form a coalition to stop him. He eventually won after three ballots.

While this book is mostly about GOP conventions, a note about the Democrat convention of 1948 is warranted here to show how ideological battles can end.

The Democrats had a deep divide in 1948 - largely over civil rights. Their primary season and convention were heated and difficult. Truman, no great champion of civil rights, nonetheless had pressed for some voting reforms and federal anti-lynching legislation that infuriated Southern Democrats.

While Truman was eventually re-nominated, he did so after a bruising match with Georgia Senator Richard Russell.

Enraged by a convention speech on civil rights by liberal icon Hubert Humphrey of Minnesota, wherein he urged the Democrats to, "get out of the shadow of state's rights and walk forthrightly into the bright sunshine of human rights," Southern Democrats didn't just sit on their hands. They walked out, forming the new Dixiecrat Party and nominating South Carolina Senator Strom Thurmond for president. This move would begin the migration of southern conservatives away from the Democrat party, cemented in the coming years through battles over states rights and the "Southern Strategy" of the Republican Party of the 1960s.

Conventions can have all sorts of impacts. On careers. On ideological direction. Even on the future of a party itself.

1976: Establishment Deals to Nomination

Throughout the 2016 cycle, pundits and prognosticators have often turned to the 1976 convention as a guide. This was the year when conservative challenger Ronald Reagan took on President Gerald Ford.

The analogy falls flat in many ways. 1976 had an incumbent. It was a one-on-one race. And it was a race that was decided through a combination of delegate tactics and pure incumbent/establishment advantage.

2016 had at its height 17 candidates, 12 or more of whom could actually have been considered serious candidates. The second tier of 2016 included the 2012 runner up and the longest tenured governor of the largest red state. That's how deep and wide the bench is in 2016.

Though the simplistic press analogies fall flat, the lessons from any tightly contested convention or race do not. While one can't simply understand the history of the 1976 convention and apply its lessons to the 2016 race 40 year later, much of what transpired is instructive.

The 1976 race had 29 primaries and 21 caucuses that year, with 2259 delegates up for grabs and 1130 needed for a victory.

Going into the convention, some reporters estimated the numbers to be 110 for Ford and 1063 for Reagan, with 94 uncommitted. John Sears, Reagan's campaign chief, openly declared he had 1140 delegates - enough to win on the first ballot. The Ford campaign seemed publicly confident, but privately frantic.

Counting delegates is something similar to counting votes in a legislative body. Some refer to it as herding cats, or to use a more colorful Texas saying, goat-roping.

There were a lot of cats and goats running around in need of herding and roping in 1976.

There were three things that became key for the Ford operation that are instructive to modern operations: First, know your delegates. Know them inside and out. Treat them like the biggest donors and the most important votes you will ever acquire, because in the case of 1976 - or any close convention- they were.

Second, have someone who is politically savvy and competent in charge of the delegate hunting and counting. Counting is important - not tabulating the totals, anyone can do that. No, counting is the skill of being able to look a person in the eye and know if they are with you, the ability not to flatter yourself into thinking optimistically about your candidate or campaign, but being able to sense what is really happening, and understanding how many delegates you actually have. Too often, even on a top tier campaign, this is an afterthought. There are precious few people with the skill and experience to do this job well. Find them early and lock them up for your campaign.

Finally — if you've got something that is legally and morally permissible to offer them to make them get into or stay in your corner, use it.

In 1976, the first two parts of this strategy fell to a political unknown at the time, who would become one of the most famous, respected political operatives of his generation, James Baker, a Houston lawyer and second tier Commerce official in the Ford Administration.

Baker would go on to run the campaign of George H.W. Bush, aid the election of Ronald Reagan in 1980, and serve as both White House Chief of Staff and Secretary of State, a distinction that puts him far ahead of most in his field.

Baker was known as both a shrewd operator and a good politician — traits that served him well in both of those later jobs — and made him especially effective as Ford's "delegate hunter" in 1976.

Baker tried to show the Ford operation some of his political instincts as the primary of his home state of Texas was being contested. President Ford had already alienated Texas voters by attempting to eat a tamale without removing the corn husks (and people think cheesesteak eating is politically dangerous!). But what he was about to do was far worse.

Secretary of State Henry Kissinger was a controversial figure in the Republican Party at this point, especially among the base voters with whom Ford was weakest. Kissinger was the leading proponent of "détente" with the Soviet Union, something that most Texans thought was French for "acting like a wimp." Needless to say, Kissinger was not popular. Yet for some reason, the Ford White House wanted to use Kissinger front and center in the campaign, something Baker (rightly) was vehemently against. In fact, he was so opposed that he supposedly ended up leaking that Kissinger wouldn't even be in the next Ford Administration.

Baker also did what any good and aspiring strategist/delegate hunter should do when they first enter a new arena or job — seek out the advice of those who did it and did it well. In Baker's case, he recounted that those who most helped him were Cliff White, who had a similar job in Barry Goldwater's 1964 operation.

Baker ran it like its own mini campaign operation, beginning with a six- page proposal for delegation management. He wanted his team to know each and every delegate in detail before the convention. The document was constantly updated and improved upon.

Both campaigns approached the convention unsure of what would transpire. Each side had successes and failures, but in the end Ford won by a hair.

How did they do it? The Ford campaign had not only professionalized the delegate hunting operation, they had also professionalized the trinkets, baubles, prizes, and the art that often goes along with backroom convention politics.

The Ford campaign used every method available. From rides on Air Force One to meetings in the White House, or calls from the President, the Ford White House was successful in its use of the presidency.

The Reagan campaign did not seem to understand the convention dynamics as well as Ford's team did, nor did they have the spoils of the presidency to offer. Instead they depended on the passion and sometimes unruly presence of the most conservative activists in America, often known collectively by then as the "New Right."

Led by luminaries such as Richard Viguerie, Morton Blackwell, Phyllis Schlafly and others, these conservative warriors brought foot soldiers that were outside the party apparatus. They weren't controlled by local or national bosses, and the White House couldn't or wouldn't touch most of them. It was an interesting set of adversaries.

Reagan made two very important mistakes in the run up to the convention. First, he didn't field a full slate of delegates in Ohio and other large states, having neither the manpower nor the money to fill out every one of them. This proved troublesome as the race narrowed. Second, he didn't contest questionable results in New York, Pennsylvania, or Massachusetts, most likely for lack of experience and lack of legal resources.

All of these factor into close races. Having a full ground game, a complete legal team, and people experienced at both can be difficult to come by if you are the outsider candidate. This type of operation normally exists only within the establishment/party apparatus. This was certainly true in 1976.

The other mistake Reagan made was to attempt to pick a moderate vice president. Reagan planned to swing two voting blocs with one move - moderate voters and delegates from Pennsylvania.

At the beginning of the convention Reagan proposed that since the race was so close, the campaigns should select their vice presidential nominees up front, so delegates could decide the nominee with the benefit of that information. Reagan chose Governor Richard Schweiker of Pennsylvania. The liberal Schweiker was seemingly an odd choice for the firebrand conservative Reagan but his calculation assumed that the Pennsylvania delegation would move to him, or at the very least liberal Republican voters might be persuaded on a second ballot.

Neither of these things happened. The Pennsylvania party chair held his delegates solid for Ford and while few, if any, moderates were swayed by this obvious political calculation, conservatives were very angry. In fact, some, led by Senator Jesse Helms, sought to draft another VP candidate from the floor.

It should be noted that everything was at stake on that first ballot. All the wheeling and dealing, all the backroom wrangling, all the perks and promises all came down to one thing: The Ford campaign suspected it absolutely had to win on the first ballot.

The binding of delegates to vote a certain way on the first ballot was on a state by state basis. A combination of Reagan delegates being bound to Ford and late momentum for Reagan in the race made it plain to the Ford people — their man was in grave danger if it went to a second ballot.

In the end, the establishment and their professional operation won — barely. It remains among the closest primary elections ever, and is the last one to go to a convention without a clear winner.

The similarity to 2016 is just that. With so many well financed candidates in the race, 2016 is the first time in 40 years where there is a real chance of that happening again. If it does, there won't be a White House using its power. There won't be one conservative candidate rallying all the troops from the outside. There will be a free for all, with four, five, or six candidates having to form coalitions and make deals.

3. THIRD PARTIES

The Tea Party is the latest in a long line of third party movements in the political arena. It is impossible to have a solid understanding of the Tea Party and its role in American politics today without understanding third party movements in history.

Traditionally, they have sprung up over a particular issue, religion, or ethnicity. While most ethnicity-based third parties lack credibility in the modern era, in the 19th and early 20th centuries, many third parties arose as a result of religious differences.

There are presently more than 30 acknowledged third parties in existence in the United States. Most of these, like the Jefferson Republican Party - a pro-life, anti-war, libertarian group that sprang from the Constitution Party - are organized regionally (in this case, the Deep South and the Far West). Others such as the Libertarians or Reform Party are more well known. Some of these parties have succeeded in electing candidates to high level positions such as Jesse Ventura who was elected Governor of Minnesota as a member of the Reform Party, but are more likely to gain visibility as distinct parties with presidential ballot access in a variety of states.

The American system is frequently called a two-party system as there are generally only two political parties with candidates running for office. The Republicans and Democrats are called "major" parties because of their ballot access, dollars raised, and existing state and local infrastructures.

The dominance of these two parties over the last 150 years is evidenced by the fact that only three members of Congress have been elected recently while not affiliated with either major party - Joe Lieberman of Connecticut, Bernie Sanders of Vermont, and Lisa Murkowski of Alaska- and all three caucused with one of the major parties in order to have influence.

The forces that incentivize the two party system (single member legislative districts, the electoral college, difficult ballot access requirements, finance compliance and disclosure, to name a few) discourage the creation and survival of third parties. Third parties are actually more successful in Europe, where multi-member districts and coalition governments enhance the power and influence of smaller blocs of legislators.

No such corollary exists in America. One of the reasons for this is the structure of our party nominating process and the winner-take-all nature of elections. However, there are examples in American history of third parties that have had major impacts on the political system.

In the early part of the 19th century, the Whigs faded into obscurity as a major party, and the Democratic-Republicans, under the leadership of James Madison, Thomas Jefferson, and their political protégés, became the Democratic Party of today. It took over 30 years from the decline of the Whigs to ultimately form what would become the Republican Party as it is known today. During that time, many third parties formed and the nation even saw the administration of an "independent" Andrew Jackson. Although he renounced his membership in the Democratic Party, it is a bit of a misnomer to label him a true independent. The structure, apparatus, and organization of the Democratic Party at the national and state level worked tirelessly to help Jackson achieve re-election. During this time, without another major organized political party to serve as a counterbalance, Democrats dominated national politics.

By 1854, however, the opposition realized it would need to be more organized and work under a single banner if it were to counteract the influence of the Democratic Party. Opposition to slavery served as a unifier among many of these third party groups and the election of 1860 became a seminal moment in American political history when Abraham Lincoln was elected as the first Republican president. In becoming the first Republican president, Republicans were galvanized as the major opposition party to the

Democrats, and helped re-establish the dominance of the two party system with the two major parties still in existence today. Most of the minor parties that came into existence after the decline of the Whigs were ultimately absorbed into the Democrat or Republican Parties by the latter part of the 1800's. Third parties in the 19th century y fall into one of three categories:

The ethnic/religious group. Nationalist/religious parties such as Irish, anti-Irish; pro-Catholic, anti-Catholic, that tended to spring up and disappear.

The single-issue group. Parties that had a single issue such as immigration or housing. whose membership would cut across ethnic and cultural lines.

The multi-issue group. All third parties have at their core dissatisfaction with the status quo- existing parties, issues, and processes. However, the parties that have lasted the longest, and functioned the best, are those that organized around multiple issues.

Examples of third parties that operated at some point during the 19th century include the Anti-Masonic, Nullifiers, American (Know-Nothings), Free Soil, States' Rightists, Unionists, Constitutional Union, Liberal Republican, National (Greenback), People's, and Silver Republican parties. Each of these parties sent members to Congress in the 1800's.

The American Party, more commonly known as the "Know-Nothings", were one of the more infamous third parties of the era. They fielded former President Millard Fillmore as their nominee in 1856, but he was soundly defeated by James Buchanan, the Democrat nominee, in a year which saw the modern Republican Party nominate their first candidate for president, John C. Fremont. The Know-Nothings were a minor party born out of a particular issue - anti-immigrant and anti-Catholic fervor. Eventually, the Know-Nothing leadership took a position advocating for the retention of slavery, a position which, apart from being on the wrong side of history, also drove a number of its members into the Republican Party, as the majority of the Know-Nothings were northerners who had come down clearly on the side of the pro-abolitionists in the Republican Party. The Know-Nothings stand as an example of a third party that grew strong enough to elect members to Congress and nominate a former president to be on the national ballot, but ultimately faltered under the weight of poor leadership.

In the 20th century, third parties were more sophisticated and nuanced in their positions, but the basic elements of their organizations remained the same. Many regional third/minor parties flourished for a time during the 1900's including the Socialist, Progressive (Bull Moose), Prohibition, Conservative, American Independent, Constitutional, Libertarian, Green, and Reform Parties. The creation of a third party is often an outlet for dissatisfaction that lends itself to a stronger two party system, as concerns around which third parties are organized are readily co-opted by one or both major parties. Over the course the 20th century, most credible third party efforts were ultimately merged into one of the two major party platforms. In this way, although the issues and geography of the periods were different, the results of third party movements of the 19th and 20th centuries were not.

More recently, the Reform Party, founded and funded by Ross Perot, made a significant impact. He was able to successfully tap into the average middle class American concern about government debt, overspending, and an unleveled playing field in the arena of foreign trade. Many of his concerns, including term limits at the federal level and a balanced budget amendment have not yet been adopted, although his presence in both the 1992 and 1996 presidential races caused the Republican Party to shift to the right and to nationalize the 1994 House elections.

You will see from the following chart the impact Third Parties have had on presidential races in the last two hundred years:

YEAR	PARTY	CANDIDATE	VOTE	EV	NEXT ELECTION
1832	Anti-Masonic	William Wirt	7.8%	7	Endorsed Whig Candidate
1848	Free Soil	Martin Van Buren	10.1	0	5%, absorbed by Republican Party
1856	Whig-American	Millard Fillmore	21.5	8	Dissolved
1860	Southern Democrat	John C. Breckinridge	18.1	72	Dissolved
1860	Constitutional Union	John Bell	12.6	39	Dissolved

1892	Populist	James B. Weaver	8.5	22	Absorbed by Democratic Party
1912	Progressive	Teddy Roosevelt	27.5	88	Returned to Republican Party
1912	Socialist	Eugene V. Debbs	6.0	0	Won 3% of the vote
1924	Progressive	Robert M. LaFollette	16.6	13	Returned to Republican Party
1948	States' Rights	Strom Thurmond	2.4	39	Dissolved
1948	Progressive	Henry Wallace	2.4	0	Won 1.4% of the vote
1968	American Independent	George Wallace	13.5	46	Won 1.4% of the vote
1980	Independent	John Anderson	6.6	0	Dissolved
1992	Reform	H. Ross Perot	18.9	0	Won 8.4% of the vote
1996	Reform	H. Ross Perot	8.4	0	Did not run
2000	Reform	Ralph Nader	2.7	0	Ran Next election
2004	Green	Ralph Nader	1.0	0	--

Although Ross Perot's 19% of the popular vote was the best showing of any third party candidate since Teddy Roosevelt in 1912, the Reform Party has faded into irrelevance as factions of the Republican Party took up some of the major concerns Perot raised during his time on the national stage.

In vying for long term longevity, third parties have a significant disadvantage in America, which transcends finance, organization, and ballot access. When a Third Party taps into an issue that motivates a large enough segment of the population so as to legitimize it, one of the two major parties will sense the momentum and absorb the issue into their own platform. Thus, the energy around that particular issue becomes split between the Third Party and the existing major party with which it most closely aligns. This is where greater financial resources, advanced organization, and ballot access come into play, and within a few cycles, if not sooner, the major party essentially subsumes the third party. Although the third party may still exist, it typically does so in name only as its members and supporters capitalize on their newfound influence within an existing major party.

This played out for the Reform Party when many of their positions were co-opted by the Bush and Clinton campaigns of 1992 and subsequently by the Tea Party more than a decade later.

This is happening again now as the Republican Party co-opts the Tea Party's principles, leaders, and activists, becoming a more conservative party as a result. But this merger will be tested significantly with the upcoming chaotic convention in Cleveland.

Will the Republican party unite after a chaotic convention, or will we see the first significant third party of the 21st century?

4. TEA TIME

Technology has transformed contemporary conservative politics more than any other single factor in recent times. However, the transformative nature first became apparent during the campaign of a candidate on the other side of the aisle. Long-shot Democratic presidential candidate Howard Dean shouldn't have made a ripple in the 2004 Democratic presidential primary, but he had a message that resonated with the base of his party, and what's more- his team was technologically-savvy. They were the first campaign team to rely primarily on the internet for raising money and organizing a national network of supporters. And it worked — for a while. Dean surged into first place, but flamed out just weeks before the Iowa caucuses. Despite Dean's collapse, campaign manager Joe Trippi emerged from the rubble of the campaign to write an entire book explaining that Dean's campaign strategy was the wave of the future.

"It was the opening salvo in a revolution, the sound of hundreds of thousands of Americans turning off their televisions and embracing the only form of technology that has allowed them to be involved again, to gain control of a process that alienated them decades ago," Trippi wrote in *The Revolution Will Not Be Televised.* "In the coming weeks and months and years, these hundreds of thousands will be followed by millions, and this revolution will not be satisfied with overthrowing a corrupt and unresponsive political system."

He was right. In 2008, then-Senator Barack Obama picked up where Dean left off. He couldn't beat Hillary Clinton just by collecting checks from the usual establishment donors and then spending the money on TV ads to reach voters. That was her game and she would win it every time. By necessity, he turned to online fundraising and social media outreach to build a grassroots machine that beat Clinton in Iowa and across the country. When the general election rolled around, Obama rejected public funding (and the cap on the amount of money he could raise in a general election) for his campaign because he knew he could raise more money from small-dollar donors.

A smaller version of the same phenomenon played out among Republicans. Ron Paul, a cantankerous, little-known congressman from Texas, didn't capture any imaginations when television and print media ruled the day. During the 2008 campaign, he combined a Dean-style anti-war message with libertarian fiscal restraint and dislike for the power brokers who control the Federal Reserve and Republican Party. It worked. He developed an internet following that turned him into a national star. He raised $28 million in 2007. About ninety percent of those donations were made online in increments of under $100. Like Dean before him, Paul couldn't turn that online support into real world victories, but Trippi had been proven more correct than he knew: an appetite for outsider politicians was growing in both parties, and the internet had given them the tools they needed to mobilize against the establishment.

Conservatives and libertarians might have taken longer than Democrats to find their Howard Dean — that is, an outsider candidate who circumvented establishment critics by using the internet to build a powerful political organization — but once they did, they didn't wait four years to take the movement national. The speed with which the Tea Party came to dominate national discourse is not it's most interesting feature. That's happened before in American politics. It's the motives of the Tea Party that make this movement unique.

As a rule, populist political movements skew left. Occupy Wall Street is a recent example, like the Dean and Obama campaigns before it. More distantly, the late 19th-century People's Party formed a coalition of western farmers and labor movements who regarded Eastern banks and railroad companies as the cause of their misfortune. The farmers who had suffered economic catastrophe through a series of droughts, wanted the government to abandon the gold standard so that they could pay their debts in the more-available silver. The 1896 Democrat nominee William Jennings Bryan gave one of the most famous speeches in American history when he thundered to a rapt Democrat Convention, "You shall not crucify mankind upon a cross of gold!" This movement called for the nationalization of the railroad companies as well. It only survived a few years, but it influenced the progressive movement and ultimately the Democratic party, so some of their policies are now familiar: they were prominent supporters of a graduated income tax, for instance.

When the Tea Party arose, the country was going through another economic crisis and the recently bailed-out Wall Street banks were certainly unpopular. But the Tea Party demanded fiscal responsibility and the restraint of government power, rather than the expansion of a progressive agenda. The broad contours of the Tea Party ideology were apparent on February 19, 2009 when CNBC's Rick Santelli uncorked the rant often recalled as the founding of the Tea Party. Santelli was outraged at Obama for "promoting bad behavior" by giving a bailout to homeowners "who can't afford the house." Had he stopped there, the speech might have been ignored as plutocratic spleen. Instead, Santelli also took a shot at Wall Street bankers by saying he would host a Chicago Tea Party and dump questionable "derivatives securities" in Lake Michigan. Crucially, he summarized his complaints about massive government spending in the economy with an invocation of the American founders. "If you read our founding fathers, people like Benjamin Franklin and Jefferson — what we're doing in this country now is making them roll over in their graves," Santelli said.

A YouTube video of the rant went viral. Web-based conservative media talked about Santelli's remarks, even as Obama and congressional Democrats exacerbated the outrage by drafting and passing a $789 billion stimulus package in just three weeks. On February 27, 30,000 people protested "taxation without deliberation" in 51 cities across the country. By April 15, the movement had grown to include about one million people.

It's hard to imagine this brand of populism catching fire at any other time, but the conclusion of George W. Bush's presidency and the beginning of Obama's tenure gave voters a strong sense of what they disliked and a belief that the rot had spread through both parties. Obama's mortgage and auto industry bailouts were consistent with the bipartisan bank bailouts of October

2008 that Bush had signed into law. Obama's stimulus package represented another expensive government intervention in the ailing economy. The overlap between the two hurt Democratic and Republican leaders alike; forty-one percent of Tea Partiers identified as either independents or Democrats, according to an April 2010 survey by the Winston Group, a Republican-leaning pollster.

Unquestionably, the chasm between party elites and their traditional political bases was wider on the right than the left. That's a consequence not just of being out of power, but how conservatives felt about their time in power. Bush left office with a 22 percent approval rating. The unpopularity of the Iraq War, Hurricane Katrina, the collapsing economy — these events took their toll among all voters, especially Democrats and independents. A president doesn't hit such historic lows without losing his base, a wound that opened in 2005. The seeds of discontent were already sown with eight years of out of control spending, but the great divorce occurred with Bush's decision to nominate White House Counsel Harriet Miers. She had served as Bush's attorney but never as a judge. Conservatives who had been burned by Republican presidential nominees before were outraged. Nobody knew her, or understood what her particular qualifications were. Bush's argument to his base was essentially, "Trust me." When that wasn't good enough the argument migrated to "Sit down and shut up." It backfired. Miers' nomination to the Supreme Court provoked as much evangelical anger as it did Saturday Night Live mockery. Harry Reid approved of the choice, but conservative media backlash was severe as elite columnists such as George Will and bloggers at National Review Online and the recently-founded RedState derided her credentials, doubted her allegiance to the social conservative movement, and denounced Bush's fidelity to the Constitution. With his polling numbers cratering, Bush replaced Miers with eventual Justice Samuel Alito. It was a move liked by the conservative base, but Bush got no credit for it. The damage was done.

This was a seminal moment for the GOP and the conservative movement, as Bush had suffered a defeat at the hands of his own political base, a base that otherwise had remained loyal in the face of relentless Democratic attacks. And the role outsider media groups like RedState and National Review Online played in the fight was also a sign of things to come.

The Miers fight had raised an existential question for Republicans and the conservative movement. "Will the Rebel Alliance abandon Bush if they can't derail Miers' nomination?" conservative writer and talk radio host Edward Morrissey wrote in October of 2015 "Some are arguing to do just that, saying it's necessary to purge the GOP of its moderates to ensure ideological purity. That still appears to be a fringe position." It was not a fringe impulse to remember "compassionate conservatism," the core of Bush's domestic policy identity, as a deviation from the truly-conservative tradition of limited government. The people who had defended Miers, voted for earmark-laden transportation bills, or insisted on the necessity of the 2008 bank bailouts while making stock market trades based on insider government information — those Republicans did not have credibility with the Tea Party conservatives. What's more, too many of they didn't seem to want it. "As soon as they get here, we need to co-opt them," former Senate Majority Leader Trent Lott told the Washington Post in July of that year. Comments like that, coming from a top Republican-turned-D.C. lobbyist, made it easy to view establishment Republicans as one part of an alliance between Big Government and Big Business to spend taxpayer dollars.

Liberal opponents of the Tea Party have long derided it as an astroturf political machine, rather than a true grassroots activist movement, but that misunderstands the nature of conservative activism, astroturf groups, or both. Every movement has individuals and organizations who "refine and enlarge the public views," to borrow from The Federalist papers, but the Tea Party movement sought leadership outside the Republican establishment. A network of bloggers, talk radio hosts and first-time political activists coordinated to host the original protests and form political groups such as Tea Party Patriots, the Tea Party Express, etc. Fox News host Glenn Beck launched the 9/12 Project. They embraced the fiscal restraint message Ron Paul had popularized in the 2008 presidential election. FreedomWorks and Americans for Prosperity, a pair of non-profits financed by libertarian billionaires Charles and David Koch, helped give the movement organizational spine.

In the run-up to the 2010 midterms, South Carolina Republican Jim DeMint guided the tip of the Tea Party spear. Elected to U.S. House of Representatives in 1999 and then to the Senate in 2005, DeMint had seen enough of GOP leadership to know that he'd "rather have 30 Marco Rubios in the Senate than 60 Arlen Specters," as he put it in 2010. And so he took the unprecedented step in 2008 of founding a political action committee, Senate Conservatives Fund (SCF), that identified conservative insurgents who could take on vulnerable establishment senators.

SCF's role in the primary process is particularly interesting: In 2010, coming off the losses of the Obama 2008 wave, the National Republican Senatorial Committee (NRSC) was looking for wins they knew were achievable. Chaired by John Cornyn and led by executive director Rob Jesmer, the NRSC made a fateful decision: they would endorse in contested primaries in an attempt to clear the field for "electable" candidates. They had no idea how much this would backfire. In Florida they felt they had scored a coup when they talked popular sitting Governor Charlie Crist into running for Senate. The price? Crist wanted a formal endorsement from the NRSC. The committee happily obliged. One problem: A young state representative by the name of Marco Rubio jumped into the race. He was a talented, energetic campaigner who the conservative grassroots in Florida loved. Soon, *National Review* put him on the cover, SCF endorsed him, and the snowball was rolling downhill. It got so bad for Crist that he actually left the GOP before the primary because he knew he couldn't beat Rubio. The NRSC was then put in the awkward position of having to support Rubio against the guy they had recruited. Rubio won handily, and Crist is a Democrat.

This played out over and over in 2010. Mike Lee got the support of the Tea Party Express and C4G against Bob Bennett and beat him in a convention. Rand Paul (Ron Paul's son) crushed Mitch McConnell's preferred candidate Trey Grayson. Pat Toomey ran against Arlen Specter (again backed by the NRSC) and Specter switched parties to become a Democrat. Specter lost the Democrat primary, and Toomey, supported by conservatives across America won. It wasn't all good news for the Tea Party though: flawed candidates in Nevada and Delaware gave away winnable Senate races.

The lessons of the 2010 election were these:

1) The days of the establishment dictating to the grassroots who their nominee would be were over

2) Technology had changed the game forever. It no longer mattered as much who the 50 big money people in a state backed. If you were a conservative who could excite the grassroots nationally, you could raise enough money in small increments to compete and win

3) The American people were ready for a more conservative kind of candidate, but they still also wanted credible, talented, disciplined candidates. While Rand Paul, Mike Lee and Pat Toomey won, Sharron Angle and Christine O'Donnell lost. This was born out in future cycles. (Think Ben Sasse and Ted Cruz.)

4) The establishment was weaker than ever. Not only was an endorsement from the NRSC unhelpful, it actually was the kiss of death for many candidates

5) The more the establishment and the media tried to big-foot the will of the grassroots candidate, the more it made the grassroots stronger. (We are seeing this play out today with Trump and Cruz.)

The rise of the Tea Party in 2010 was a seminal moment in American politics. To regard the leaders of the Tea Party as astroturf puppeteers is to malign them with their own success and ignore the circumstances that made it possible. Jim DeMint was a little-known backbencher before he founded SCF. David Koch's Libertarian Party vice presidential bid went nowhere in 1980. Ron Paul's success could not be predicted by his abortive 1988 campaign. But the failures of the Bush administration and the overreach of the Obama team conditioned a broad swath of the American voting public to be receptive to the fusion of libertarian and conservative ideals that has always characterized the Republican Party at its strongest. Senate Minority Leader Mitch McConnell, to his credit, kept Republicans united against Obamacare at a time when many liberal Republican lawmakers wanted to cooperate with Obama. That set the stage for the Tea Party to channel its energy into the GOP and sweep Nancy Pelosi out of the House Speaker's office.

Don't believe the revisionist history: You can't fake a wave election.

5. DISRUPTIVE CAUSATION

The end of the brokered convention era didn't occur by happenstance. The growth of televisions in homes across America meant that voters had a seat at the convention, and they didn't like what they saw. As a result, Republican Party leaders deftly changed the rules over time to put more emphasis on primary contests and less emphasis on smoke-filled back room deals between sometimes questionable characters.

Although over time the party leaders took power away from themselves and put it in the hands of voters through primary elections, they maintained control over the levers of power that allowed them to have an outsized role in persuading voters to implement the outcome they desired. But now in a primary process that is dominated by outsider momentum, those party bosses have lost control.

Just as television changed the process from brokered conventions to media conventions, new disruptive technologies are leading us from media conventions to contested conventions. It isn't that voters want a convention fight, but rather that there has been a rebellion in the grassroots against the establishment that has been effectuated by a number causes and will ultimately lead to a chaotic convention fight.

Cause 1: Open-source Campaigns

The decentralization of technology allows candidates and political movements to organize, raise money, and impact elections in ways that weren't possible just a decade ago.

Technology has disrupted almost every major industry in America and campaigns are no different. New technologies have broken the ability of consultants and political parties to control campaigns and have allowed new consultants who understand these emerging technologies to thrive. In turn, this has allowed candidates who are not supported by the establishment to over-perform.

A prime example of this is how, beginning in 2010, national Tea Party candidates began to emerge by using the internet to engage small dollar donors from across the country to fund their campaigns, moving outside the realm of large campaign donors and bundlers controlling the flow of campaign dollars.

Open-source in the world of development generally means that code is available for people to use and manipulate. In this book we extrapolate on that meaning to include the use of several tools such as phone calls, online advertising, email lists, television advertising, data modeling, data structures, and other systems that have been made available through open source code and also through the natural decentralization that occurs through technological development.

Open-source campaign means building a political campaign from the ground up, allowing grassroots activists to essentially take control from the wealthy financiers, party bosses, and other political professionals who formerly controlled the tools prior to open-source and decentralization of technology.

In previous cycles, grassroots activists were confined to stuffing envelopes, putting up yard signs, and responding to direct mail solicitations for small contributions. Their role became less and less important because mailhouses essentially made campaign mail stuffing obsolete, yard signs are of questionable effectiveness as a persuasion tool, and postage costs have made direct mail a terribly inefficient method of donating money to a particular candidate.

However, the emerging open-source nature of political campaigns has now revolutionized American politics to the point where Rand Paul, Ted Cruz, Mike Lee, Christine O'Donnell, and Sharron Angle can upset the preferences of party bosses and their establishment consultants.

Open-source means that a few consultants can no longer control the process.

1) TV ads no longer require tens of thousands of dollars for production. When I was John McCain's Political Director in the 2008 presidential primaries, many of our TV ads were produced by a young, yet very talented, campaign operative on his laptop in the corner of the campaign headquarters.

2) Polling can now be done very inexpensively by Interactive Voice Response (IVR) and is arguably as effective as traditional live polling, especially for tracking surveys. Again, the McCain campaign in the 2008 presidential primaries utilized high volume IVR for polling in ALL early primary states. The Romney campaign also utilized IVR in 2012 and probably every presidential campaign is using IVR In 2016 (with the possible exception of Trump). This is a dramatic change from 2008 when very few candidates managed by leading consultants used IVR – in fact they ridiculed it.

3) Fundraising can now be done online, and millions of dollars can be raised almost instantaneously if grassroots support for a candidate exists. For example, Christine O'Donnell raised $3.5 million online in a matter of days after she was shunned by Karl Rove and the NRSC the night of her primary victory. More recently, Ben Carson has led the field in terms of fundraising in almost every quarter of the 2016 presidential campaign, largely as a result of online donors.

4) Campaigns now use free tools such as Google Calendar, Facebook, Twitter, and other programs to organize their campaigns. Every campaign uses a Customer Relationship Management (CRM) tool to organize their contacts, and most campaigns have databases that are relational to the tools that are used to contact voters.

What this means is that campaigns are no longer dependent on the kingmakers of the process. Grassroots activists across the country are now the ultimate kingmaker......not the party bosses or the billionaires.

Cause 2: The Rise of the Tea Party

The rise of the Tea Party has given campaigns the manpower needed to effectively challenge the establishment and provided a new spectrum for decision-making other than a strictly ideological one.

The rise of the tea party has already been thoroughly described in this book, but it is essential to understand the impact that the rise of the Tea Party will have in the context of a contested convention.

Party contests used to be won based on momentum. Candidate A gathered some initial support and the snowball grew bigger and bigger as the campaign moved forward and rolled down the hill.

The very nature of establishment campaigns meant that people would want to support the winner and therefore party leaders would select which candidates would win contested party races. It was a self-fulfilling prophecy. The establishment guy was going to win because he had party support, and he had party support because he was going to win.

But the Tea Party created exactly the opposite effect- candidates popped up in response to an establishment trying to dominate the process. Whereas being an outsider used to be a negative, today there are a substantial number of activists participating in the party process who will almost automatically oppose the establishment candidate. This has been playing out in House and Senate races for the last three cycles.

All of this history is important as we think about Cleveland. The dynamics that will dominate this convention didn't start yesterday. This battle has been brewing since 2010 and the outsiders have the momentum.

Cause 3: Wide Open Field

A wide open Republican field of candidates with no heir apparent that began with 15 credible candidates for president.

The 2016 Republican field of candidates is the strongest and most diverse field of candidates in modern times.

The field can be broken down into three main lanes: establishment, outsider, and social conservative. Those lanes can then be broken down into ideological sub-lanes such as conservative/moderate/libertarian.

Establishment Lane

The establishment lane includes several candidates trying to appeal to traditional GOP primary voters on the establishment side of the spectrum. There are candidates who are working from the conservative side of the establishment lane, and others who have placed themselves in the center-right, or moderate, side of the establishment lane.

Marco Rubio - Marco Rubio won election in 2010 against establishment-backed moderate Charlie Crist with the help of outside groups such as Club for Growth and SCF. But after winning the election he quickly distanced himself from the outside groups that helped him win and severely tarnished his conservative outsider brand by helping to lead the Gang of 8 immigration bill with liberal Democrat Chuck Schumer. He has competed more for the establishment lane by hiring more establishment-minded (yet very talented) consultants such as Terry Sullivan to run his operation and more significantly, they have made an effort to publicize his support from more moderate billionaires within the party. Yet Rubio's team has attempted to place him on the conservative side of the establishment lane, despite his moderate baggage on immigration. They seem to be convinced they can unite the establishment and outsider spectrum behind his candidacy.

Jeb Bush - It is perhaps impossible to be any more establishment than a candidate with the last name Bush. The Bush family is the most well respected and successful Republican political dynasty in modern times. Moreover, Jeb Bush's tone is a moderate tone of respect and inclusion rather than a bomb-throwing tone of anger and blame. Jeb Bush was clearly operating from the more moderate side of the establishment lane in the early phases of the contest, but has more aggressively highlighted his conservative record in Florida in later stages.

John Kasich - John Kasich was a conservative in Congress who cut spending and balanced budgets. He governed more as a moderate in Ohio in passing and defending Medicaid expansion in his state. He hired the well-respected center-right consultant John Weaver to help run his presidential campaign and largely avoided Iowa to attempt a New Hampshire-centric path to the nomination. He fits well with traditional New Hampshire primary voters and independents who bolstered John McCain in 2000 and 2008. Kasich has a very conservative record to run on but is operating from the center-right side of the establishment lane.

Outsider Lane

The outsider lane includes candidates who are trying to appeal to GOP primary voters who on the on outsider side of the spectrum. It is very difficult for a currently elected official to be more outsider than Donald Trump or Ben Carson because they have never been elected to office before and were not previously viewed as politicians.

Ted Cruz - Ted Cruz spread himself relatively thin in trying to compete in the liberty lane, outsider lane, and social conservative lane in order to try and put together a winning coalition. He competed with Rand Paul early on to try and appeal to liberty-leaning voters with his positions on surveillance and skepticism on engagement in the Middle East, but over time has presented himself as more hawkish in response to the rise of ISIS and attacks from Marco Rubio. Whereas Rubio quickly moved towards the establishment after winning election in 2010, Cruz stuck with his anti-establishment credentials. He continued to work with outside groups such as SCF and, in fact, resigned his position on the NRSC when there was a conflict. It would be hard to be more anti-establishment than Ted Cruz and he would have a lock on the outsider lane if it wasn't for Donald Trump and Ben Carson. He has also done an excellent job reaching out to social conservatives who will have a big role in southern states and beyond.

Donald Trump - It is significantly easier for someone who has never been elected to office to be able to bottle the anti-establishment fervor that has swept the country. Rick Snyder did it as a relative moderate in Michigan, Curt Clawson did it as a conservative in Florida, and Ben Sasse did it as a conservative in Nebraska. Donald Trump is doing it as well as anyone in history. He has turned out to be a talented politician who is in tune with the base on the most important issues of the day such as immigration, and is almost perfectly navigating and downright dominating the daily news cycle. He is as big of an outsider as you could ever have in a presidential race. It is interesting to note that ideologically he seems to pull from moderates and conservatives relatively equally.

Ben Carson - Ben Carson did an excellent job grasping the anti-establishment fervor that swept the country and raised record amounts of money from small donors who were inspired by him. It remains to be seen if there is room for him on the outsider spectrum with Ted Cruz and Donald Trump competing for similar votes. He is operating from the social conservative side of the outsider lane.

Social Conservative Lane

The Pat Robertson campaign of 1988 brought millions of new social conservatives into the party. They were once viewed as the outsiders within the party but over time- as always happens in a two party system- a major party co-opted their issues. The Republican Party simply became more socially conservative, and over time social conservatives began to dominate the party, essentially becoming the insiders within the party structure (with the exception of the socially moderate major donors who are often determinative in the establishment lane selection process).

Mike Huckabee and Rick Santorum have dropped from the race at the time of this writing, but it is worth noting that in previous cycles they would have been viewed as social conservative outsiders. In this cycle, with more clarity in the outsider lane coming from candidates such as Ted Cruz, Donald Trump, Ben Carson, and Rand Paul, they didn't own much space in the outsider lane. And they certainly didn't own any space in the establishment lane because, by definition, the establishment and its donors would never accept them.

Mike Huckabee - Mike Huckabee should have been a much stronger candidate in Iowa but the outsider candidacies of Trump and Cruz simply dominated the discussion- and more importantly- won over social conservatives.

Rick Santorum - Rick Santorum shared the same fate as Mike Huckabee as a highly credible and qualified candidate who was never going to garner the attention of the more bombastic outsiders.

Cause 4: The New Spectrum

The disruption of open-source campaigns, rise of the Tea Party, and libertarian participation have led to the dominance of a new outsider spectrum.

It was once easy to predict who a person supported for a particular office by estimating where the person was on the ideological spectrum relative to the candidate. The ideological spectrum as taught in Political Science 101 classes at universities across the country was a two-dimensional spectrum that has liberal on the left and conservative on the right Libertarians argue that the spectrum should be three dimensional, with liberty also represented.

IDEOLOGICAL SPECTRUM

3-DIMENSIONAL IDEOLOGICAL SPECTRUM

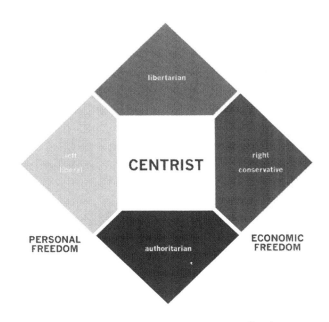

www.conventionchaos.com

The capabilities of open-source campaigns and rise of the Tea Party have evolved the the two-dimensional or three-dimensional ideological spectrums. A new and more dominant spectrum has emerged in the decision-making of donors, activists, voters, and candidates across the country: The outsider spectrum.

The outsider spectrum is based on where someone is on the the outsider vs. establishment divide. It is largely a self-classification and based on rhetoric, however it is unique in that whether or not you were previously elected is a dominant variable in your placement on the spectrum.

It is hard for someone who hasn't been elected to be establishment, and even harder for someone who has already been elected to be an outsider.

OUTSIDER SPECTRUM

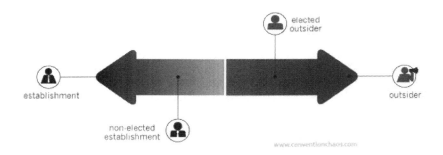

The outsider has won the vast majority of highly contested primary contests over the last six years since campaigns went open-source and the Tea Party movement emerged. Sharron Angle, Christine O'Donnell, Todd Akin, Ben Sasse, Ted Cruz, Rick Snyder, Curt Clawson, Mike Lee, and numerous others defeated establishment backed candidates in tough primaries across the country. There were a few establishment wins such as Mitch McConnell, but the very notion that the establishment has to mention the Senate Majority leader winning a primary is testament enough to the strength of the outsider band of the spectrum.

The strength of outsiders has been demonstrated in spades in the 2016 primaries with Ben Carson leading the field in fundraising, Donald Trump leading the field in polling, Ted Cruz considered a favorite for the nomination, and yet successful Governors such as Scott Walker, Chris Christie, and Bobby Jindal, struggled.

Cause 5: Libertarian Participation in the GOP

Libertarian participation has increased within the Republican Party electorate, which has led to less stability in the grassroots state conventions across the country and far less ability for state-based party bosses to control local GOP elections.

One of the most important things the Tea Party did electorally in terms of Republican internal politics is that it helped in reuniting libertarians and conservatives while appealing to independents and disaffected Democrats.

Ron Paul helped in convincing libertarians to participate in the Republican electorate, and dramatically grew the number of liberty-leaning Republicans as a result of the 2008 and 2012 campaigns for president. These new activists are not necessarily loyal to the Republican Party, and certainly do not follow the recommendations or guidance of the GOP establishment and its allied operatives, nor do they respond well to establishment threats. For example, actions by the McCain and Romney campaigns, RNC, and their supporters at the 2008 and 2012 national conventions seriously risked liberty-leaning participation and support for Republican candidates. This arguably hurt GOP chances for winning the general election.

But overall, the inclusion of libertarians in the Republican Party dramatically increased the number of anti-establishment participants in Republican State Conventions, and at the Republican National Convention.

More importantly, the involvement of these new activists seemingly scared the Republican establishment into making significant rule changes at the that are backfiring and will lead to the first multiple ballot convention in modern times.

Cause 6: RNC Rules Changes

Rules changes simultaneously made national convention ballot access more challenging and made it more difficult for candidates to win a majority of delegates by encouraging more states to go proportional rather than winner-take-all.

The Republican Party vastly overreacted in 2008 and 2012 to the inclusion of libertarians in the grassroots process.

They changed the manner in which rules were enacted by allowing the RNC to adjust the rules after the 2012 convention, they made national convention ballot access more difficult for presidential candidates, they enacted rules that resulted in less states being winner-take-all, and they instituted a chaotic balloting situation resulting from the binding of delegates.

Their response to these charges is that they can once again change the rules before the 2016 convention. But the convention Rules Committee will be made up of convention delegates who are more loyal to the candidates they support than they are to an outgoing RNC Chairman. In fact, any effort to change the rules by the establishment will likely backfire even further.

Regardless of how they try to fix the mess, the changes in rules that were made in 2012 made a contested national convention much more likely, and a chaotic national convention unavoidable.

Cause 7: Diversification of Media and Proliferation of Social Media

The diversification of media took power away from television executives who favored more establishment-oriented candidates. The proliferation of social media took power away from major donors and party leaders. Both of these causes increased the political opportunities for candidates who would not have been able to survive past the early states in previous cycles.

The disruption of the media industry by technology has created a significant diversification and decentralization of the media. The first big step in this process was arguably the founding of Fox News by Rupert Murdoch and Roger Ailes in 1996. This provided the conservative perspective in much the same way that CNN provided what conservatives viewed to be the liberal perspective previously. The next big steps were the founding of Facebook in

2004 and Twitter in 2006 that connected the world and created instant communication and organization between friends through social media.

Suddenly people communicated ideas directly with one another, unfiltered by the mainstream media, and no longer had to rely on powerful television and newspaper corporations for their information. This allowed open-source campaigns to become much more powerful, and allowed the Tea Party to effectively communicate, inspire, and recruit like-minded supporters.

This reduced the power of television news, and also dramatically reduced the potency of television advertising. The reduction in the effectiveness of television advertising became apparent as super PACs wasted hundreds of millions of dollars on network television ads in the lead-up to the 2016 presidential nomination contests.

It also reduced the authority of party bosses because the party activists who previously received most of their information from their party leaders were now able to gather the information for themselves. This increased the authority of grassroots activists who were given more tools to gather information and think for themselves.

The combination of all of these dramatic changes, precipitated by the decentralization of media, flattened the the presidential nomination process and helped take power away from the establishment GOP. This made a contested and ultimately chaotic national convention more likely.

Cause 8: Dramatic Increase in Online Fundraising

The increase in online fundraising as a proportion of overall receipts and velocity of donations relative to older fundraising techniques gave more conservative candidates with anti-establishment appeal a mechanism to fund campaigns with millions and millions of dollars from smaller donors.

Online fundraising began in real terms with John McCain winning the New Hampshire primary on February 1, 2000. His campaign wisely put his domain name both on the banner above his head and on the podium sign while he was speaking. Nearly $1 million was raised that night online by small donors across the country who were invigorated to try and defeat the Bush establishment. This was the first outsider challenge of the establishment in the internet age and arguably began the era of open-source campaigns.

Online fundraising continued to grow from election cycle to election cycle at a relatively gradual rate until the formation of the Tea Party when anti-establishment fervor swept the country.

Anti-establishment candidates such as Sharron Angle, Christine O'Donnell, Allen West, Ted Cruz, and numerous others were able to raise significant amounts of money online largely by utilizing anti-establishment rhetoric to galvanize conservatives who were upset by the spending policies of George W. Bush, scared that newly-elected President Barack Obama was pushing our country towards socialism, irate about the proposed national health care policy, and most importantly, tired of establishment Republicans who lacked the strength to stand up and oppose the direction our country was headed.

Since 2010, online fundraising from small donors has been funding many, if not most, successful primary campaigns across the country. This has dramatically reduced the power and authority of bundlers, billionaires, and party leaders who would previously seek to implement their will over campaigns and operatives by impacting the relative fundraising revenues of various campaigns and party committees.

Simply put, anti-establishment candidates and operatives no longer need to care what the establishment thinks. This is apparent in the early stages of the 2016 contest with outsider Ben Carson leading the field in fundraising with the help of hundreds of thousands of small donors.

Cause 9: The Evolving Role of Super PACs

Super PACs have the power to keep candidates in the race long after, historically, they would have been forced to drop out, while simultaneously super PAC ads have experienced reduced effectiveness.

Although online fundraising radically decentralized the power of campaigns from high-powered campaign financiers down to grassroots activists and online fundraising consultants, the advent of super PACs simultaneously gave a very wealthy individual the ability to keep a campaign running long past the time it normally would have shut down from lack of resources.

The natural life cycle of a campaign previously meant that the candidate was in the race until they ran out of money. But the ability of a billionaire to put money into a super PAC allowed candidates such as Newt Gingrich to stay in the 2012 presidential race after his campaign stopped raising enough money to compete in contests.

This dramatically upset the natural life cycle of a campaign, and kept more campaigns in the race for much longer. Almost every campaign in the 2016 cycle is heavily reliant on a super PAC to spend money on voter contact such as television, radio, mail, and telephone campaigns to persuade voters. Several of those campaigns probably would have dropped out of the race much earlier - even before the Iowa Caucuses - if the super PACs weren't helping their campaigns. And there will almost certainly be campaigns that are kept alive by super PACs up until the national convention in Cleveland.

Cause 10: The Proliferation of Outsider Groups

The proliferation of outsider groups such as Tea Party Express, Tea Party Patriots, Senate Conservatives Fund, Club for Growth, Americans for Prosperity, and others have given outsider candidates more resource firepower than ever before, provided a training ground for outsider operatives, and facilitated list building and software development.

Several new conservative outside groups have gained strength as a result of the Citizens United ruling that opened the door for political action committees that do not coordinate expenditures with campaigns to accept unlimited donations.

Most of these groups have emerged on the conservative anti-establishment side of the spectrum. As a result of the rise of many of these groups, for the first time, the grassroots have had the ability to fight the establishment on nearly equal footing and win. Below is a discussion of some of the most influential outsider groups:

Americans for Prosperity (AFP) - AFP was founded in 2004 when Citizens for a Sound Economy (CSE) broke into two groups: AFP and FreedomWorks.

AFP receives substantial funding from the influential businessmen Charles Koch and David Koch and has been widely credited with helping to transform and invigorate the Tea Party movement with resources and organizational assistance. AFP was the leading organizer of many of the initial Tea Party events held across the country in 2009-10.

Today, they have chapters in every state, and hundreds of thousands of activists nationwide who receive their messaging and can be deployed to contact voters at a moment's notice at the federal, state, and local levels.

In 2009, in response to the bailouts and the impending passage of Obamacare, AFP helped rally the conservative base across America to go to town hall meetings and tell their congressman that they opposed what the administration was doing. Liberals have tried to dismiss this uprising as "astroturf" (a fake movement with paid people) but the results simply do not bear that out. It's true that AFP put resources into building an organization, but the people they found were real, were often acting on their own time, and were very passionate about limited government.

Unlike so many conservative groups that in years past focused all their efforts on Washington, AFP is heavily focused on the states. In 2009, AFP launched a "Porkulus" campaign at state capitols across the country. In April of that year, they led a "Tax Day Tea Party", a movement protesting Obamacare, the so-called stimulus, and other wasteful government spending. This was just a foretaste of what was to come in 2010. AFP was instrumental in harnessing that energy of 2009 and carrying it over to the ballot box in the midterm elections. They spent over $40 million on rallies, ads, and registration drives. By any calculation, AFP played an instrumental role in handing Barack Obama the worst loss of his political career. They weren't done there. In 2011, AFP went all in to help Wisconsin Governor Scott Walker stave off a recall by angry unions. Today, AFP remains one of the most important conservative groups in the country, with a massive network of activists.

FreedomWorks (FW) - FreedomWorks was also founded in 2004 following the breakup of CSE. FreedomWorks merged with Empower America and had a powerful trio of Dick Armey, Jack Kemp, and C. Boyden Gray as Co-Chairmen. Shortly thereafter, Steve Forbes joined as well.

Similar to AFP, FreedomWorks also played a pivotal role in organizing the Tea Party rallies of 2009 and helping to turn that energy into conservative victories in 2010. They were instrumental in the 9-12 Tea Party March in 2009 in which hundreds of thousands of Americans marched on Washington in protest of Obamacare and the stimulus. For those who were there, it was an unforgettable day. Up to that point, many conservatives had felt frustration at the losses of 2008, and the seeming helplessness to stop the Obama Agenda. But that Saturday morning was massive. People from all across the country, many of whom had never been to a political event in their lives, showed up in force. From that moment, it was clear that the Tea Party was going to be a major force in American politics.

Today, FreedomWorks endorses candidates in primaries, conducts trainings, and arms activists with materials. Along with AFP, they have the biggest activist network of any group on the right.

The next three groups are different from the two already discussed in that their focus is specifically on electing conservative candidates. They have been involved in the election of just about every conservative senator and congressman of the last few cycles.

Senate Conservatives Fund (SCF) - SCF started as the PAC of U.S. Senator Jim DeMint of South Carolina and run by Matt Hoskins. It has become the preeminent anti-establishment campaign organization in the country. SCF focuses on helping conservative, yet electable, candidates win U.S. Senate primaries. They were initially formed in 2008 when DeMint, a long time back bencher who had been a relatively good soldier, grew frustrated with the leadership of Mitch McConnell and the willingness of GOP leadership to surrender to Democrats, decided to form his own organization designed to elect conservative candidates in primaries. 2010 was SCF's first big year, helping elect candidates like Marco Rubio, Rand Paul, Pat Toomey, and Mike Lee, despite the protests of McConnell and the National Republican Senatorial Committee. They built on 2010, playing a pivotal role in the election of Ted Cruz in 2012 and Ben Sasse in 2014. After DeMint left the Senate and relinquished control over SCF in 2013, the group started targeting moderate incumbents as well, coming within a hair of taking out Thad Cochran in Mississippi in 2014. They raise millions of dollars for anti-establishment candidates and spend millions more on their behalf. Without them, the Tea Party would not have nearly as many victories under their belts.

Club for Growth (C4G) - Founded in 2004, the C4G has long been "the bad guy" on Capitol Hill as far as career politicians are concerned. They are unafraid to publish scorecards highlighting bad votes by politicians regardless of party. They don't care if you are a Republican or Democrat, if they don't like how you voted, you will hear from them. The Club has a long history of fielding candidates to mount primary challenges against moderate Republicans, and have long been considered a thorn in the side of the establishment. In 2008, they hammered Mike Huckabee on his moderate economic record in Arkansas, and this year, they have spent millions attacking Trump for insufficient conservatism.

In 2010, they spent almost $9 million on behalf of candidates, and bundled almost that much directly to campaigns. They remain one of the biggest dogs on the conservative block and should be feared by any establishment Republican who votes for higher spending.

Tea Party Express (TPE) - TPE is another group that focuses heavily on helping anti-establishment challengers take on heavily favored moderate, establishment candidates and win. They have a list of hundreds of thousands of conservatives across the country that they can mobilize at a moment's notice. When they come to town, people know about it, and they have provided many a momentum boost for a Tea Party challenger when they needed it most. They have a rare combination of grassroots activists on the ground and voter contact online and through the air that most other organizations lack.

It used to be that being a governor was seen as having an advantage in reaching the White House, and that being in the Senate was something of a political graveyard. Not since Jack Kennedy had a senator been elected until Barack Obama came along. So it is interesting to note that looking at the candidates in the presidential race this year, (Marco Rubio, Ted Cruz, Rand Paul, etc.) many of them had fought the establishment and won big races that they were not supposed to win. Why is that? Because powerful outside groups like SCF, C4G, TPE, all weighed in for these guys early, and made them famous among the conservative grassroots. To these small dollar donors, Ted

Cruz isn't just a random senator, he's the guy who took on the Texas establishment and won. You could say the same about many of the others-they're guys who anti-establishment conservatives have rooted for, donated to, and fought. They are literally invested in every one of these candidates. It's no coincidence that each of them have been some of the highest profile members of the senate and are beloved by the grassroots. None of that would have happened without the groups investing in them early. Those battles in senate races the last three cycles have shaped everything we see happening today.

The impact of these groups can also be felt in the development of operatives. The campaign manager for Donald Trump, the leaders of the Ted Cruz Super PAC, several television production gurus, and other key operatives cut their teeth and rose to prominence by taking on the establishment through these outside groups.

There is also better software being developed because the establishment vendors don't control all the development dollars, better lists being built because outside money can be spent on list development, and more lessons learned because group-think is becoming obsolete as outsiders challenge conventional wisdom.

Cause 11: Establishment vs. Tea Party/Outsider Role Reversal

The past few decades the Republican electorate had a majority establishment-leaning center-right coalition that was able to unite behind one candidate and use the invisible primary to drive other similar candidates from the race. On the other hand, conservatives had a minority of the national Republican electorate, and tended to divide their respective chunk of the electorate up among multiple candidates. The roles have reversed.

The establishment previously - almost by definition - could implement their will and consolidate the number of candidates in a race. They would systematically get all available fundraisers in line and on the team, then use grassroots leaders to get all the key grassroots activists on board, convince their friends in the media that the race was over as a result of that success, and ultimately cut off the supply of oxygen and money to other potential campaigns. This is sometimes referred to as the "invisible primary."

Perhaps the best example of this is the Bush campaign in 2000. George W. Bush received the endorsement of more than two thirds of the RNC, almost every Republican governor, and a significant proportion of Republican members of Congress from across the country. He revolutionized hard dollar fundraising by branding bundlers as Pioneers and Rangers. Only a self-funder such as Steve Forbes was able to put up a serious fight before New Hampshire, and that led to him spending millions of dollars and only winning ten delegates to the national convention.

But now with online fundraising, the decentralization of media, the rise of the Tea Party, and other reasons previously discussed in this book, there has been a role reversal between the establishment and the anti-establishment sides of the party.

Whereas the establishment used to get each other in line to support their preference, now there are at least four candidates fighting for the establishment lane.

Whereas the establishment used to make up a majority of voters, all the establishment candidates combined receive a minority of support among the GOP electorate compared to outsiders Donald Trump, Ted Cruz, and Ben Carson.

Whereas the establishment always led in fundraising, the fundraising leader in this campaign has been Ben Carson - a doctor who had never run for office before and has practically no endorsements from known political leaders.

The anti-establishment side of the spectrum now has greater unity, more money, and more voters than the establishment.

This reversal of roles means that there are more candidates who have the ability to run campaigns all the way to the Republican National Convention in Cleveland.

Cause 12: Death of the Invisible Primary

The death of the invisible primary caused more outsider candidates to be able to compete in the early stages of the campaign process because the endorsement game no longer matters.

The book Game Change was largely told from the perspective of people who came into the McCain campaign relatively late. Steve Schmidt's role was largely a messaging role in talking to the candidate on the phone until the primaries were won. He was not given day-to-day control of the McCain campaign until July 2008.

The McCain presidential campaign actually began more than four years earlier at the 2004 inauguration of George W. Bush. The next two years were fought as an aggressive proxy war between the Romney and McCain campaigns wherein they would distribute money, endorsements, and other forms of support to candidates for local and national office across the country.

Some might argue that the campaign actually never ended after Bush defeated McCain in 2000, and played out as a Bush vs. McCain battle in primaries across the country in the years 2000 to 2004. Others might argue that the stage was set in June 2004 when McCain declined John Kerry's entreaties to be his running mate on the Democrat ticket. This led to many Bush loyalists including Terry Nelson, Nicole Wallace, Rob Jesmer, Jon Seaton, and others joining an early incarnation of the McCain 2008 team.

But there is no arguing against the fact that the invisible primary was alive and well between John McCain and Mitt Romney in 2005. McCain donated $50,000 in 2006 to local Republican parties throughout Michigan, and similar amounts in other important states across the country. Romney responded by donating roughly the same amount to similar organizations. McCain and Romney would hire operatives left and right almost as an excuse to put out a press release proclaiming the hire rather than to actually get real help in winning the nomination.

The world changed. There was seemingly no invisible primary in the 2012 election- there was a new paradigm. Rather than try to demonstrate a majority of establishment support, the new battle was emerging as to who could maximize the energy of Tea Party voters across the country.

Gone were the endorsement releases and consultant hirings that dominated the previous cycles. This was a new world, and everyone was trying to get their sea legs to see what it all meant.

In 2016, some might argue that the Walker and Bush presidential campaigns initially waged an invisible primary war through hirings that put the Walker campaign out of business, much like the McCain campaign had nearly been put out of business eight years earlier. Participating in an arms race when you don't have the ability to print money is a dangerous game to play in national campaigns.

The Rubio campaign deserves kudos for not getting dragged into this losing battle and instead waiting for the real fights of 2016.

With the possible small exception of Walker vs. Bush, in many ways the 2008 proxy battle between McCain and Romney was the last presidential campaign in modern history where the candidates for president competed to win the invisible primary by releasing endorsements and buying the party structure. In short, the party no longer decides.

The book *The Party Decides* written by Marty Cohen gave an accounting of how and why the establishment gained power through invisible primaries:

> Throughout the contest for the 2008 Democratic presidential nomination, politicians and voters alike worried that the outcome might depend on the preferences of unelected super delegates. This concern threw into relief the prevailing notion that—such unusually competitive cases notwithstanding—people, rather than parties, should and do control presidential nominations. But for the past several decades, The Party Decides shows, unelected insiders in both major parties have effectively selected candidates long before citizens reached the ballot box.
>
> Tracing the evolution of presidential nominations since the 1790s, this volume demonstrates how party insiders have sought since America's founding to control nominations as a means of getting what they want from government. Contrary to the common view that the party reforms of the 1970s gave voters more power, the authors

contend that the most consequential contests remain the candidates' fights for prominent endorsements and the support of various interest groups and state party leaders. These invisible primaries produce frontrunners long before most voters start paying attention, profoundly influencing final election outcomes and investing parties with far more nominating power than is generally recognized.

The invisible primary is dying, and that means that candidates who don't have the support to compete in the invisible primary won't be pressured out of the race for losing it. This gives an advantage to outsider candidates and keeps more campaigns running up to the national convention.

Cause 13: Donald Trump and Ted Cruz

The establishment usually figures out a way to agree on most everything. But they can't seem to agree on who they dislike more- Ted Cruz or Donald Trump. Regardless, the two frontrunners scare the establishment, and their success ensures that we will have a contested convention.

Donald Trump is a candidate who the establishment loathes and will do anything to stop. He simply doesn't care about any threats the establishment could ever make, and he doesn't have donors and key supporters who could persuade him to do anything "for the good of the party." He will do what he thinks is right.

Ted Cruz is arguably in an even worse position when it comes to his relationship with the establishment. Donald Trump might not care what they think, but Ted Cruz has historically seemed to poke them in the eye and enjoy it in the process.

The establishment will do everything in their power to stop both of them, and that includes fighting their nomination all the way to the convention, manipulating the rules of the convention, and throwing the convention into total chaos.

Cause 14: Home State Heroes

There is a long history in contested conventions going back to the 1800's of candidates running as essentially one-state candidates to represent their home state, control those delegates, and use that political capital on the convention floor as negotiating power.

There are only nine states that are winner-take-all and therefore there are limited opportunities to win a majority, rather than plurality, of delegates in a state. Two of those states are the states of Ohio and Florida. There is a good chance that John Kasich wins Ohio regardless of how well he is doing at that point in the contest. This would give him a large number of delegates and control of a state delegation. Similarly, Jeb Bush or Marco Rubio have a good chance of performing well in Florida regardless of how well they are doing in other states at that point in the contest.

Both of these states could provide momentum to the winner for later contests, but more importantly for the purposes of this section, there is a strong possibility that the number of winner-take-all states that are available for a frontrunner to win could be further limited.

This provides additional pressure on the ballot access requirement of a majority of eight states. It is harder to get a majority of eight states if home state heroes win two of the nine states that are winner-take-all.

The uncertainty around ballot access will encourage more candidates to stay in the race longer and participate in the brokering that might take place. This potentially leaves more candidates in the race longer and increases the chances for a contested convention.

6. The Path to Chaos

The causes of a contested convention have now been described at length. But what is the path to a contested convention?

Until recently the Republican Party almost always nominated the guy who came in second the last time. Reagan ran in 1976, but won the nomination in 1980. Bush ran in 1980, but won in 1988. Dole ran in 1988, but won in 1996. McCain ran in 2000, but won in 2008. Romney ran in 2008, but won in 2012.

But this time Rick Santorum hardly received 2% of the vote in Iowa as the runner up in 2012. Everything has changed. The party no longer rewards past service, nor is it a predictor of future success.

The Path to Chaos: Tea Party >> Outsiders >> Win
Following the 2010 and 2012 Tea Party losses, the Democrats and establishment Republicans did a good job of branding the Tea Party in such a negative way that it turned off independents and many Republicans.

However, the spending policies of George W. Bush, the economic collapse of 2008, the nomination of John McCain, the selection of Sarah Palin, and the election of Barack Obama combined to give conservatives and many independent voters an adamant 'throw the bums out' attitude.
The rise of the Tea Party gave grassroots organization to the unrest across the country, but it also gave the naysayers an opportunity to vilify and negatively brand the Tea Party.

As a result of the attacks on the Tea Party, and the failures of some of the candidates associated with the Tea Party, the movement's polling numbers dropped over time.

Do you consider yourself to be [a supporter of the Tea Party movement, an opponent of the Tea Party movement], or neither?

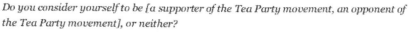

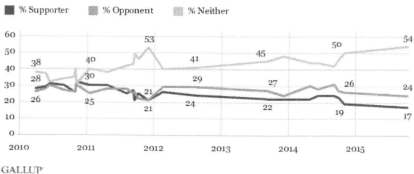

GALLUP

Despite the branding problems that the Tea Party has faced in recent years, the fact is that outsider candidates still outperform insider candidates in primary elections across the country, and do remarkably well in general elections. It is no coincidence that successful candidates today run as 'outsiders' rather than Tea Party candidates.

The Path to Chaos: Campaign Examples
There have been a number of primary campaigns since the rise of the Tea Party in 2009 that are important in understanding the path to a contested convention in Cleveland.

Essentially, there has been a civil war playing out in campaigns across the country with the establishment on one side and outsiders on the other. For example:

- Sharron Angle 2010 Nevada US Senate primary
- Christine O'Donnell 2010 Delaware US Senate primary
- Todd Aiken 2012 US Senate primary

- Rick Snyder 2010 Michigan Governor primary
- Ted Cruz 2012 Texas US Senate primary
- Curt Clawson 2014 FL-19 Congressional primary
- Ben Sasse 2014 Nebraska US Senate primary
- State Convention Fights Across the Country

Example 1: Failed Candidates and Failed Establishment Response to Failed Candidates

Sharron Angle was a firebrand conservative who earned support for her Senate run from outside groups such as C4G and TPE, after her years in the Nevada legislature.

The 2010 election cycle was by far the most problematic and vitriolic cycle between the establishment and anti-establishment forces within the Republican Party.

Candidates across the country were able to raise large sums of money and garner significant voter support by (fairly or unfairly) condemning Karl Rove, Mitch McConnell, John Boehner, the NRSC, and any other Republican leader or institution that could be branded part of the dreaded establishment.

Meanwhile, establishment operatives hadn't yet figured out that they were now the enemy of the grassroots base of the party, and continued the flawed tactics of overreaction, threats, and ridicule.

This led to a lack of cooperation between a campaign that was largely run by locals with no serious campaign experience, and a national party committee that had not yet learned how to deal with the new world where being in power was viewed very negatively.

The result was several losses such as Sharron Angle and Christine O'Donnell that otherwise could have been won in a cycle that turned out to be a tidal wave for Republicans.

Example 2: Establishment Incompetence Breeds Distrust

Campaigns are an imperfect science. All candidates make mistakes. There is no strategist or staffer who is immune from making mistakes either. This is partially because decisions aren't made in a vacuum and there are actions and reactions based on every significant decision. It is often said that campaigns are a game of three-dimensional chess rather than checkers.

Tea Party campaigns tend to make more mistakes than traditional campaigns because they tend to have inexperienced candidates who hire inexperienced people and put them into significant roles.

However, the failures by the establishment in recent years have also handicapped the party at large. In 2008, the RNC failed to match the technology of the Obama campaign, and the Romney campaign of 2012 made every attempt not to make that mistake again. But instead, they failed much more spectacularly and ultimately lost the confidence of grassroots Republican activists. The volunteers who worked hard to help Mitt Romney get elected were frustrated on election night in 2012 by the failures of Project ORCA.

Project ORCA was a relatively secret project by the Romney campaign that used technology to track voter turnout on Election Day and give the campaign an opportunity to move resources where needed. Conceptually it was a good idea that many campaigns have attempted over the years as technology has improved. But it froze on Election Day probably because it had not been properly stress tested.

Grassroots Republicans were outraged by what they learned in the news reports and headlines that followed the losses in 2012.

Romney's fail whale: ORCA the vote-tracker left team 'flying blind'
- Politico 11/08/12

Romney's ORCA program sank
- Politico 11/09/12

Inside Team Romney's whale of an IT meltdown
- Arstechnica 11/9/12

Inside Orca: How the Romney Campaign Suppressed Its Own Vote
- Breitbart 11/8/12

The Romney Campaign's Ground Game Fiasco
- The Daily Beast 11/9/12

Why Romney's Orca killer app beached on Election Day
- CNET 11/9/12

Daily Caller 11/16/12
"As of Friday, 10 days have passed since the Romney campaign lost the presidential election for Republicans, and the makers of the campaign's over-hyped and extremely secretive Project ORCA election reporting tool are still nowhere to be found."

ORCA is probably the most spectacular failure in campaign management in the modern era of Republican campaigns. Some people argue that the failures of ORCA cost Mitt Romney the election, but that is highly unlikely at best. Regardless the establishment was blamed for a high-profile failure.

Tea Party activists lost faith in the establishment for their failures just as quickly as the establishment lost faith in Tea Party candidates who lost.

It is easy to give the establishment the benefit of the doubt and say that if candidates such as Sharron Angle and Todd Aiken were winning general elections then they wouldn't fight them so hard in primaries. Similarly, it is a congruent argument that if the establishment hadn't failed so spectacularly with ORCA in 2012 then grassroots activists across the country might have more confidence in the establishment's ability to run competent campaigns.

These examples demonstrate why the divide between the establishment and outsider segments of the spectrum are also based on competency rather than just ideology or experience.

Example 3: Outsider Spectrum as Dominant Variable

In the 2010 Michigan Governor's race Rick Snyder started at zero percent in the polls and knew almost no one in the GOP. He was moderate in tone and unwilling to use the hard-core conservative rhetoric that other Republican primary candidates often use in GOP primaries across the country. Plus, he was running at a time when the Tea Party was founded, peaked, and won contested primaries across the country. Yet he overwhelmingly won a contested GOP primary election against a very strong field including a sitting Attorney General, a powerful congressman who held a committee chairmanship, a sheriff of the most important electoral county in the state, and the sitting Secretary of State.

More interestingly, he was the most moderate candidate in the field who released endorsements from known moderates such as former Governor Bill Milliken, former Congressman Joe Schwarz, and businessman Bill Ford. He even ended the primary campaign with an ad that featured a Democrat saying that they were a Democrat who was going to crossover and vote in the GOP primary for Rick Snyder (Michigan has an open primary).

Despite this ideological positioning, the crosstabs in the exit polling showed that Snyder won Tea Party voters.

Why? Because he was an outsider, not part of the GOP establishment.

Tea Party voters weren't necessarily ideological. Some were conservatives, but some were also disgusted Democrats and independents. Simply put, they wanted to throw the bums out and stop the same old politicians from being recycled into a new office.

The lesson is that you could appeal to Tea Party voters, independents, and disaffected Republicans by running as an outsider rather than running as a Tea Party candidate.

2010 GUBERNATORIAL PRIMARY ELECTION

CANDIDATE	VOTES	%
RICK SNYDER	381,327	36.4
PETE HOEKSTRA	280,976	26.8
MIKE COX	240,409	23.0
MIKE BOUCHARD	127,350	12.2
TOM GEORGE	16,986	1.6
	1,044,925	100

www.conventionchaos.com

Example 4: Good Candidates Matter

It is an oversimplification to argue that races can be decided simply based on the relevant spectrums. Campaign consultants and operatives like to argue that "campaigns matter." While that is true, it is also true to say that candidates matter. There is no substitute for a good candidate running a good campaign.

Two of the best candidates who ran the best campaigns in the country in 2014 were Curt Clawson and Ben Sasse.

Curt Clawson in FL-19

Curt Clawson had recently moved to southwest Florida after running a worldwide Fortune 500 company.

His parents lived in Bonita Springs and he moved there to be closer to them. While he was there he became concerned about some environmental policies and took an interest in politics. He was a conservative businessman who viewed the environment as critical to southwest Florida's economic comeback and ultimate success.

When Congressman Trey Radel resigned from office, the FL-19 congressional seat opened up. The GOP establishment was getting behind State Senate President Lizbeth Benaquisto. In fact they took it to the extreme. The Republican Party of Florida transferred money into a super PAC that ran attack ads against Clawson in the primary. Plus, the NRCC started an effort to recruit more women to run for Congress that took sides and helped Benaquisto raise money. Both of these actions are almost unheard of – the state and national party directly getting involved in a primary election. But both of these efforts backfired and only brought attention to the narrative that Curt Clawson was an outsider taking on the establishment.

Curt Clawson hadn't identified with the Tea Party previously, but essentially agreed with their national organizations on the issues, and certainly thought the Republican leadership in Washington was failing.

Curt Clawson ran as the outsider for Congress. His Twitter handle was OutsiderClawson. The word "outsider" was in his logo. The campaign ran TV ads showing him hitting 3-point basketball shots from long range to visually demonstrate his outsider status.

He won the election in a blowout by 12 points in a four-way race against very tough competition.

2014 SPECIAL FL-19 SPECIAL ELECTION

CANDIDATE	VOTES	%
CURT CLAWSON	26,857	38
LIZBETH BENACQUISTO	18,032	26
PAIGE KREEGEL	17,762	25
MICHAEL DREIKORN	7,560	11
	70,211	100

www.conventionchaos.com

Curt Clawson is a perfect example that running as an outsider can inspire support of Tea Party conservatives without having to say the controversial things that were said by previous unsuccessful Tea Party candidates across the country.

Good candidates matter.

This is also another example of the establishment trying to manipulate the primaries and having it backfire.

Ben Sasse in Nebraska US Senate

Ben Sasse was an unknown but a tremendously intelligent and talented president of a small college in rural Nebraska. He had worked in the Bush administration and was friends with a wide range of establishment leaders.

Despite his personal connections to members of the establishment, he didn't like the direction of Washington insiders and was a tremendously articulate spokesperson for the conservative movement. He didn't necessarily think of himself as Tea Party, but he certainly didn't agree with the establishment on how government was functioning. He thought like an outsider.

The campaign released an ad that literally talked about moving the capital from Washington, D.C. and showed it on a Mack Truck headed towards Nebraska. There was no better way to express distaste for the dysfunction in Washington than to argue - even if tongue firmly planted in cheek - for moving the U.S. Capitol to Nebraska.

He was clearly the outsider. Now he had to publicly become what he already was privately: the conservative outsider. He ran ads saying that he was one of the few people who had read the Obamacare legislation word for word and knew how to dismantle it. He was endorsed by outside groups including C4G and SCF, among others. FreedomWorks initially endorsed his opponent but then switched their support to Sasse later.

This race clearly demonstrated that you didn't need to say stupid things in order to earn the support of Tea Party activists. Instead, you could run as an articulate and intelligent outsider who was willing to take on the status quo in Washington, D.C. and still win the election.

Conservatives who want an electable, ideas-based leader in 2020 would be wise to consider Ben Sasse if Republicans don't win the presidency in 2016.

Once again, good candidates matter.

Example 5: Ideological Spectrum as Dominant Variable

The outsider spectrum is usually dominant over the ideological spectrum – as shown by Donald Trump in 2016 and by Rick Snyder in 2010 – but there are times when an establishment-leaning candidate can appeal to outsiders based on conservative ideology.

John Moolenaar in MI-4

The Moolenaar race is a little different in that John Moolenaar tended to vote with the establishment on procedural matters in the Michigan State Senate, but almost always voted hard core conservative when it mattered, including voting against Governor Snyder's Medicaid expansion.

His opponent was a highly qualified wealthy businessman named Paul Mitchell who was self funding. Despite being an outsider and running against someone who was arguably an insider as a State Senator, Mitchell never established his outsider credentials.

Moolenaar aggressively reached out to the establishment by earning the endorsements of outgoing Congressman Dave Camp and State Attorney General Bill Schuette. Moolenaar had a strong conservative voting record in the State Senate and was able to parlay that into support from Senator Mike Lee, Rick Santorum, the Tea Party Patriots, TPE, and other outsider groups.

John Moolenaar proved that an experienced elected official with a very conservative voting record can establish outsider credentials and defeat and outsider businessman even in this difficult climate. The roles can be reversed. Good conservative candidates can win the support of outsider groups on ideological grounds.

Example 6: Michigan State Conventions

Michigan is unique in that grassroots Republican activists have a larger role in the nomination of statewide elected officials than in any other state in the country.

The Michigan Republican Party selects its nominees for Lt. Governor, Attorney General, Secretary of State, and University Board positions at its nominating convention. Roughly 2000 GOP activists are elected to be state convention delegates at county conventions across the state. The convention even nominates candidates for nonpartisan judicial positions on the Michigan Supreme Court.

The convention also selects the Michigan Republican Party Chairman, Republican National Committeeman, Republican National Committeewoman, and other statewide Republican Party officer positions.

This makes the Michigan GOP Convention the dominant vehicle for contested fights within the Michigan Republican Party and as a result, convention contests, rather than statewide primaries, tend to define the party from cycle to cycle. Michigan state conventions provide an excellent microcosm of what is paying out in intra-party battles across the country.

1988 Michigan GOP State Convention
The presidential election of 1988 was a seminal moment in national GOP history and brought hundreds of thousands of new social conservatives into the Republican party through the Pat Robertson campaign. This was very similar to what is happening today with the influx of Tea Party conservatives into the party.

The Michigan Republican Party decided to allocate their delegates in 1988 through a state convention system rather than through a presidential primary. The convention was in January – before even the Iowa caucuses.

It was a critical battle in the war between the George H.W. Bush establishment, the social conservative insurgency of Pat Robertson, and Jack Kemp who was inspiring to many Reagan-conservatives. It would help determine the direction of the nominating process and directly challenge the perceived grassroots strength of the Robertson social conservative organization.

The state convention was a watershed moment that would define the future of the post-Reagan Republican Party. The momentum and insurgencies were similar to today, but there were also mechanical similarities.

There were rules fights.

There were credentials fights.

There were fights to decide who would run the state convention.

And ultimately, after Chuck Yob was elected Chairman, the Robertson and Kemp people walked out and held their own "rump convention" in another room.

All of this played out on live national TV.

But ultimately the establishment controlled the convention and won the delegates for George H.W. Bush.

Some would argue that the 1988 state convention was thrown into chaos.

The results of the 1988 convention defined the Michigan Republican Party for the next ten years, with John Engler firmly in charge of the party following his election to governor in 1990.

Imagine what would happen if this same thing played out on the national convention stage in Cleveland.

Total chaos.

1998 Michigan GOP State Convention

"To really get Michigan's political landscape, you have to go back eight years, to the 1998 race for Michigan attorney general. In one fell swoop Yob defeated Governor John Engler in a major political battle, screwed Mitt Romney's brother Scott out of an easy election to state office, and came to be blamed for costing Republicans the next governor's election." - 6/24/2006 Weekly Standard

The Michigan Republican State Convention in 1998 and the intraparty struggle that followed were emblematic of what happened nationally in the lead up to the Tea Party movement of 2009-10.

While the Tea Party movement brought in many new people to the political process, much of the organizational muscle behind it came from people who had been involved in the Republican Party in the past.

Many of the Tea Party "leaders" that emerged had been involved in previous decades, lost recent elections, or been shut out by establishment party leaders. These were people who had been in electoral or local party battles in previous cycles but didn't necessarily have the troops to be successful. But suddenly the Tea Party movement provided millions of new people to participate in the process and ultimately to defeat many local GOP party machines across the country.

A big part of this is the establishment handling things poorly in both victory and defeat.

The 1998 Michigan GOP State convention was a battle between "the grassroots" and "Engler." Jon Smietanka had been the Republican nominee for Attorney General in 1994 and had run a relatively strong campaign, but ultimately was not victorious.

Engler wanted Scott Romney to be the nominee in 1998, thinking that Romney would be a stronger general election candidate given his family's storied history in the state and ability to fundraise.

Chuck Yob was the Republican National Committeeman from Michigan and had a very strong relationship with the grassroots base of the party. He had served as County Chairman and District Chairman in the Grand Rapids area, and was elected National Committeeman in 1989. He had been active in the party in several other areas of the state and had traveled the state helping local parties set up local fundraising operations. He had generally prioritized returning phone calls from precinct delegates and genuinely cared about their concerns. He was the grassroots.

He had run for RNC Chairman the year before and had an instrumental role in the election of Jim Nicholson as RNC Chairman.

Yob had previously been somewhat of a conduit between Governor John Engler and the grassroots base of the Republican Party and had generally helped Engler implement his preferences at the convention.

But in this case he was not willing to help shove Smietanka to the side, and it became a battle of the conservative grassroots versus the more moderate GOP establishment.

Smietanka won the convention, but lost the war.

After Smietanka's victory at convention the divide in the party was clear between the grassroots base and the loyalists to Governor Engler.

Governor Engler had made the point strongly that Smietanka would be defeated in the general election and he was proven correct. However, his mistreatment of the people who supported Smietanka proved to create a movement against him and other establishment leaders in the state that continued for a decade.

In many ways, 1998 was the beginning of the anti-establishment wave that transformed into the Tea Party movement in Michigan. Every Michigan Republican battle over the next 10 years was fought over whether you were an Engler (establishment) person or a Yob (grassroots) person. The Yob organization was successful in turning the anti-Engler rebellion into a long-lasting tribe that fought together for over a decade and won most contested conventions including multiple races for statewide office. He became almost unbeatable in a convention fight.

The Smietanka fight, and the fights that followed, framed the battle within the Michigan Republican Party up to the 2009-10 rise of the Tea Party, and many of the people who supported Smietanka ended up being participants in today's anti-establishment efforts in Michigan.

There are many lessons from this convention that can vary significantly based on your perspective. But it is hard to argue with the fact that the anti-establishment side lost the general election and the establishment overreacted – causing damage to their efforts for years to come and strengthening their opposition.

The 2010 Michigan State GOP Convention

The 2010 Michigan Convention was the first meaningful convention after the rise of the Tea Party and took place just a few short weeks after Rick Snyder won the Republican nomination for governor.

The delegates weren't happy that the more moderate candidate had used his outsider status to defeat more conservative candidates in Mike Cox, Pete Hoekstra, and Mike Bouchard.

There was considerable unrest in the convention hall. This was partly because the establishment was overplaying their hand and trying to implement their will over the convention. It culminated with a rambunctious and difficult Rules Committee meeting on the morning of the convention where the establishment was trying to change the rules to give an advantage to incumbents over non-incumbents in the University Board races. They were specifically trying to protect an incumbent MSU Trustee against outsider Mitch Lyons, a former NFL and Michigan State University football player.

The establishment won the battle but winning that battle cost them the war. The anti-establishment side left the rules meeting very upset and put out word through their whip operation that the establishment had changed the rules and were cheating. That message was reinforced in the nominating speeches and Mitch Lyons won with an overwhelming victory.

But it almost had much worse consequences in the races for Attorney General and Lt. Governor. The race for Attorney General ended up much closer than some people anticipated, and there was nearly a significant challenge for the position of Lt. Governor with the newly nominated Snyder.

It is clear that the establishment trying to change the rules at the last minute backfired and gave momentum to the anti-establishment side of the spectrum. This is an important lesson as the national convention Rules Committee convenes in July.

The Path to Chaos: The Lessons of These Examples

There are many lessons to be learned from these examples and they naturally vary based on your perspective. However, there are some that are worth pointing out again:

- Failed candidates set back the Tea Party movement substantially, but the establishment response to those failed candidates was arguably even more damaging to the future of the party.

- Establishment incompetence breeds distrust among grassroots conservatives in much the same way failed Tea Party campaigns bother the establishment.

- The outsider spectrum may very well be the more dominant variable in the equation of primary electability than the ideological spectrum, but it is still possible to reach out to Tea Party voters on ideological grounds

- The evolution of the party, losing campaigns, and establishment response to losing campaigns, has placed greater emphasis on nominating good candidates.

- Convention fights can define the party for subsequent years or decades and bringing the team back together after a contested convention can be determinative of the future success of the party and its candidates.

- Using the power of the establishment to change the rules can easily backfire and can lead to momentum against those in power. It is easy to win the battle yet lose the war.

7. The Tribes

One of the untold stories of political operatives, and especially of presidential campaigns, is the role of tribes in the campaign process. There are tribes of operatives who tend to work together, and there are tribes of operatives who tend to work against each other. And of course there are operatives who just plain despise each other.

Political consulting and campaign management is a tribal business and operatives tend to be a member of one tribe or another. This means that operatives have friends in the business who try to hire each other, pay each other as vendors, share in the spoils of victory, and express loyalty to one another when the chips are down. They also often share common enemies among competing tribes.

Part of the reason for the tribal aspect of the industry is simple in that people tend to work with people who they know. If you work with someone once, and it goes well, then you might want to work with them again. There is nothing negative or nefarious about working with people who you have had success with in previous contests - experience is a good thing.

But there is also competition and in some cases downright hatred among the individuals. They work against each other when they pitch candidates, badmouth each other in attempts to win business, and refuse to use various vendors to prevent them from entering the marketplace.

The political marketplace is not an efficient market where the cream rises to the top automatically. Instead, it is a very difficult marketplace to break into with self-interested consultants who work against each other and show favoritism for their preferred vendors and products.

The most well-known example of a vendor helping to build a tribe is FLS Connect. FLS was formed in the lead up to the Bush 2000 campaign and continues to be the dominant phone vendor on the Republican side today. For example, Jeff Larson, the "L" in FLS, is now the CEO of the national convention. Rich Beeson, a partner at FLS, is the Deputy Campaign Manager for Rubio's presidential campaign. David James, the Political Director for Jeb Bush, is also a partner at FLS.

It doesn't take a Masters Degree in Campaign Management to figure out that those three guys will be talking at the Republican National Convention and when the chips are down they won't have a hard time trying to figure out a way to work together. This isn't to infer anything inappropriate.

This is important from a national convention perspective because there are members of various tribes who are also currently working on opposing campaigns.

The Tribes: Trust
It is critically important to be able to trust the person with whom you are trying to cut a deal or otherwise work with on the convention floor. There are countless stories of very high profile people and operatives making deals in high pressure situations such as party elections and nomination contests only to fail to keep their end of the bargain after winning. Having people on your campaign who have worked with people on the opposing campaigns is critically important in a multi-candidate field convention contest where dozens and dozens of deals are going to need to be cut by the winning campaign.

Deals could range from something as high-profile as a vice presidential promise, to agreeing to strategic voting on the floor, or working together in the election of delegates at state conventions, or in electing committee members among the respective delegations.

The first case of this will come about in the state convention delegate selection process. Campaign operatives will be cutting deals with each other such as "we can't win Michigan's convention but we have some state delegates there that we will ask to vote for you, if you ask your state delegates in North Dakota to vote for our folks instead of yours. You know you can't win North Dakota's national delegates anyway."

The second case of this will come about in the process of electing members of the committees of the Republican National Convention. Each state delegation will need to elect members of the various committees, and various campaigns will work together in that process in order to get a working majority in that state. For example, two candidates who have a majority of delegates could team up to stop any other candidate from getting any supporters elected as committee members in a particular state.

The third case will be once the convention committees meet.

The various campaigns will be cutting deals with each other on critical credentials challenges that will literally change the makeup of the convention delegates in a few states. And there will be plenty of coordination when it comes to updating the rules on critical matters such as delegating binding.

But the most important deal-making may be as it relates to ballot access. Multiple candidates who earn delegates in contests during the primary and state convention phase are unlikely to reach the minimum threshold for ballot access at the national convention. Therefore, they will try to barter these delegates with the other campaigns if the final convention rules allow it. In some cases, this will be just friendship and acceptance as a close ally. In others, it will be specific jobs for various high level people, potentially including the candidate.

The Tribes: Networks

The tribes all began somewhere. There is always a high profile campaign, party organization, consulting company, or cause that united allies, making it attractive to work together in the future.

CRNC Tribe: The College Republican National Committee (CRNC) is perhaps the longest-running and most successful tribal network in Republican politics. The CRNC is a very serious political organization with tens of thousands of members and a budget of millions of dollars. Past CRNC leaders include Lee Atwater, Karl Rove, Ralph Reed, Grover Norquist, Morton Blackwell, Patrick McHenry, Brock McCleary, and Michael Davidson among other well known political operatives.

Every competent CRNC Leader uses their time there as an opportunity to build a national political network that can be put to use in future national campaigns.

Karl Rove dropped out of college in 1971 to serve as Executive Director of the CRNC and successfully utilized the organization to build a loyal network of operatives in most of the 50 states. There was a great deal of discussion about the Bush family network being put to work for George W. Bush, and that was true, especially on the finance side. But on the political side Rove also built his own operation that relied on people who he had met in College Republicans (CR's) over the years. For example, Bob Kjellander, the Republican National Committeeman from Illinois, and David Tyson, the State Chairman of West Virginia, were both friends of Rove from the College Republican days and later key supporters of Bush on the Republican National Committee. There are hundreds - or even thousands - of similar examples across the country.

I ran for CRNC Chairman and my campaign manager was initially Patrick McHenry, who is now a well-respected member of Congress from North Carolina. I served as General Chairman and Executive Director of the CRNC in 1999.

My first CRNC Convention included US Senator Richard Shelby getting thrown out of the Credentials Committee meeting for asking questions of the Credentials Committee. The Credentials Committee were all appointed by the CRNC Chairman and therefore whoever the CRNC Chairman supported always won CRNC elections. The establishment literally rigged the elections.

The reason Senator Shelby was escorted from the Credentials Meeting was because he had the gall to question why it was appropriate for the establishment states to be able to use the student school phone directory as their list of members. The argument that was given was because all CR Members are listed, and although some people who aren't members were also listed, there was nothing precluding them from submitting non-members in their list as well.

We spent the next few years trying to clean up the election process and I am proud to say the CRNC now has an honest elections process void of controversy. This was a crash course in fighting the establishment, and indeed they readily admit today that they had their fingers on the scales.

The friends that I built at the CRNC helped John McCain in the 2008 nomination victory and in several other races across the country.

Bush Tribe: The most well known tribe in American politics are "The Bush People" and date back at least to 1970's activities of George H.W. Bush, if not before.

Karl Rove's network that dated back to the College Republican days helped build the infrastructure for the George W. Bush campaign in 2000. It is also noteworthy that Karl Rove had been a part of the Bush tribal network in his earliest days as a political operative. In fact, RNC Chairman George H.W. Bush essentially chose Karl Rove as Chairman of the CRNC after a convention that had its results appealed to the Chairman of the RNC.

But the Bush network was being built long before Rove was a member of the CR's. George H.W. Bush served as Congressman, Ambassador, RNC Chairman, Director of the CIA, Vice President, and President.

McCain Tribe - The McCain operation had many iterations of tribes. The first McCain tribe was run by John Weaver and Mike Dennehy and included the people who fought George W. Bush and Karl Rove tooth and nail throughout the 2000 election cycle. Their campaign staff never got very big but they did have some loyal soldiers in states across the country.

After McCain declined the vice presidential nod from John Kerry, the McCain operation essentially co-opted part of Karl Rove's Bush team with the help of Terry Nelson. Terry Nelson was offered the Campaign Manager job for the 2008 presidential campaign sometime in 2005 and was introduced to the political operative class as a McCain guy at the Colorado Springs RNC Meeting. For the next two years, a large segment of the Bush tribe became the McCain tribe. Terry Nelson was brought in as Campaign Manager. Nicole Wallace was brought in for high-level Communications. Rob Jesmer became National Political Director. Jon Seaton became National Field Director. The traditional McCain people of Rick Davis, Christian Ferry, Mike Dennehy and others were pushed to the side in favor of the Bush Tribe. This lasted until 2007 when Terry Nelson and John Weaver abruptly quit and Rick Davis was put back in charge. Literally dozens of staff immediately quit and left no records behind for the new political operation.

The leftover McCain folks - minus the Bush people - pulled off the most dramatic presidential primary campaign comeback in Republican political history. Never before had a candidate gone from frontrunner to long shot and back to victor in the nomination process. The political team that won was Rick Davis, Christian Ferry, John Yob, Bo Harmon, Jim Barnett, Buzz Jacobs, Ryan Price, Jordan Gehrke, Adam Meldrum, and others.

But once again the tribe changed and for whatever reasons the Bush people were put back in charge. Steve Schmidt didn't want to be perceived as disloyal to Terry Nelson and the rest of the Bush tribe and therefore he and John McCain essentially hid the fact that they were communicating even after the Bush tribe exited the McCain campaign. Although Schmidt had little to do with campaign operations during the primary, he had McCain's ear and a dominant role in campaign messaging for a campaign that was devoid of pollsters. He assisted with the motto "Country First" and the position of doubling down on the Iraq surge that proved successful in the primary process. McCain referred to Steve as Sergeant Schmidt, and their relationship was very much one military man to another in terms of their non-verbal communications. Simply put, no one was able to connect with John McCain like Steve Schmidt.

Steve Schmidt was named Campaign Manager in July of 2007 and Mike DuHaime was brought into the campaign to run political operations.

DuHaime had an excellent reputation – especially in Bush circles - but had just run a less than successful campaign for Rudy Giuliani that bet all their chips on the Florida primary rather than New Hampshire.

The Bush Tribe was once again firmly in charge of the McCain campaign for the general election. Most of the political operation that had won the nomination was moved over to run the Republican National Convention in Minneapolis.

Other Tribes – There are dozens of other tribes in Republican politics including previous RNC political staff, Romney staff, and Ron Paul Staff. There are also state based tribes such as in Michigan, consultant based tribes across the country, and many bundlers have effectively built their own tribes in the finance world. (The examples given in this book are nowhere near an exhaustive list of tribes. These just happen to be the examples that are closest to the author.)

The Tribes: Impact on RNC

A major source of the disagreements between the establishment and anti-establishment operatives stem from the attempted blackballing and obvious favoritism that happened at the RNC before the open-source era.

There are famous stories of the Bush people blackballing the McCain people after the 2000 election. Similar things have occurred throughout history and continue to this day.

Chairman Reince Priebus has made significant strides towards reaching out to other vendors and operatives and not allowing the RNC to get trapped in vendor personality fights. Priebus is generally an honest broker and fair person who wants what is best for the party and tends to be more conservative than most professional operatives.

Progress is clearly being made at the RNC, but the tribal impact remains.

The Tribes: Impact on Trump

It is a fool's errand to try and guess who is going to win, place, or show in each state, but it seems pretty clear that Donald Trump is going to perform well and win delegates across the country.

Donald Trump is also the one candidate that most of the establishment and campaign consulting tribes will team up to work against. You can bet that when the chips are down the establishment tribes will unite. Donors, operatives, and supporters of the establishment candidates will at some point unite to try to defeat Mr. Trump, and he will be somewhat at a disadvantage because of the tribal connections.

Simply put, they will try to screw him over big time in Cleveland.

8. The Presidential Campaigns

Presidential campaigns are organized chaos. Even the most successful campaigns are unable to do everything that they would like to do. Most are unable to do even half of what they would like to do. So every campaign needs to focus on the strategy that they think can help lead them to victory despite limited time and resources. The old saying everyone "has a plan until you get punched in the nose" is very true.

Some campaigns have a 1-State Strategy like McCain 2000 focusing on New Hampshire and McCain 2008 eventually focusing on New Hampshire again. Rick Santorum focused on a single state- Iowa- in 2012.

Some campaigns have a 2-State Strategy that focuses on Iowa and New Hampshire, and others have a 3-State Strategy that focuses on Iowa, New Hampshire, and South Carolina.

Very few campaigns ever have the time and resources to allocate to a national convention delegate strategy. It is a lot more expensive than a 1-State Strategy, or a 2-State Strategy, or even a 3-State Strategy. The only campaign in modern times that seemed to have a serious and well funded national convention strategy during the early primary contests was Ron Paul.

Most of the campaigns are doing the work of getting their supporters to run for national convention delegate, but very few if any campaigns are investing resources into properly preparing for a contested convention. But in order to get a sense of what kind of work the campaigns are doing to prepare for the national convention, you need to understand the people in charge of building the campaigns and what makes them tick.

Do the strategists truly believe in investing in the grassroots, or do they believe that television ads determine outcomes?

Do the strategists believe their candidate can actually win, or are they just trying to over-perform?

The hiring of a campaign manager, consultants, and key staff has changed dramatically over time as the technology and media environment have changed.

One of the first questions to ask about a campaign is which department the campaign manager comes from:

- If the campaign manager is a former TV consultant, then you can bet that most of the money will be spent on TV and that the consultant commission might be a variable in the decision-making process.

- If the campaign manager is an older wise man who has been around campaigns since the 1970's, then you can bet that the campaign will be slow and methodical, make few mistakes, but not get much accomplished in a faster moving world.

- If the campaign manager is a fundraiser or major donor, then you can bet that decision-making is based on the whims of the donor community, for better and/or worse.

- If the campaign manager is a former Political Director, then you can bet that there will be strong phone, mail, and field organizations.

- If the campaign manager is a Communications Director, you can bet most decisions are made in the context of what will win or overachieve in the news cycle.

- If the Campaign Manager is an online strategist, then you can bet many decisions will be in the context of online acquisitions of email addresses, online fundraising, and social media.

- If the Campaign Manager is a convention operative, there is a good chance they will be prepared for state conventions across the country.

The people who the candidates hire to run their operations are even more important in the convention process. The value of an individual in a primary process is both talent and connections. But the value of connections in a convention process is exponentially higher than it is in the primary process.

It is much easier to navigate the waters of ballot access, filing delegates to run in the states, and ultimately to compete at state conventions in the delegate selection process if you have connections or a tribe in the states where you are competing.

But connections are only part of the game. You also need to fundamentally understand state and national conventions. There are very few operatives in the country who understand the concepts in this book and even fewer who have them memorized and can construct them into a winning strategy that includes smart tactics to maximize the rules and systems to their favor.

The team you put together for early states might be far different than the team you need at a convention fight.

The Trump Campaign

The Trump campaign has resisted the temptation to follow the traditional roadmap of spending money on television ads and putting together a strong field operation to turn out the vote. They achieved remarkable success in 2015 and the early stages of 2016 despite spending only around $5 million.

It remains to be seen whether their reluctance to engage in traditional campaign systems will delay them in putting together an experienced team capable of winning state convention fights to get the right delegates elected and help them win the contested national convention. Mr. Trump is obviously a very smart man and so it is likely he will sooner or later build a convention team that is second to none.

Trump Campaign Manager: Corey Lewandowski

It is hard to argue with success. Corey Lewandowski is perhaps the most important and least well known operative running a presidential campaign as we head into a contested convention in Cleveland. He was previously National Director of Voter Registration for Americans for Prosperity (AFP). He also served as Campaign Manager for Bob Smith for U.S. Senate, and as an assistant for Citizens for a Sound Economy (CSE).

He has strong New Hampshire ties that served Trump very well in the New Hampshire Primary, as well as connections with other outsider operatives across the country.

There is a significant advantage to knowing people in other states across the country who you have worked with before. You could argue that AFP is in the early stages of building a tribe that Lewandowski is utilizing to help Trump. Several state-level operatives formerly worked for AFP.

The Trump campaign has been a well oiled machine so far and Corey Lewandowski deserves credit for that, and the benefit of the doubt that he will eventually put together a strong convention operation.

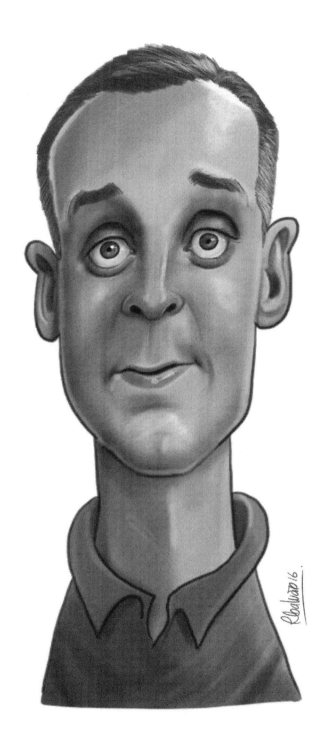

Trump National Political Director: Michael Glassner
Michael Glassner is a political pro with decades of experience working for everyone from Bob Dole to George W. Bush to Sarah Palin.

There is little doubt that he knows what he is doing and will do what it takes to build a team capable of effectively battling at a contested national convention.

The Cruz Campaign
The Cruz campaign is a conglomeration of mostly conservative outsider operatives who haven't been accepted by the establishment for one reason or another.

This is not to say they are not successful. Some of the most successful consultants in the industry - both electorally and financially - have come from the outsider and conservative sides of the spectrums rather than from the moderate establishment.

They tend to believe in grassroots organizing and in the new power of big data for high-level voter targeting, and utilize cutting edge tools to build online organizations that can be turned into on the ground field teams.

Cruz Campaign Manager: Jeff Roe
Jeff Roe is an experienced political consultant who usually handles multiple high profile candidates at a time with an emphasis on middle America. He specializes in strategy and mail but fundamentally understands the levers of campaign management at all levels.

His experience in running state and national convention is unclear but it should be assumed he will put together a first rate convention team.

Cruz Advisor: Saul Anuzis

I have had a history full of friction with Saul Anuzis. Regardless of how you interpret those battles, Anuzis is one of the more talented operatives and leaders in the Republican Party.

Personality matters in convention politics because you meet and interact regularly with the people who are working with, and even the people you are working against. This serves Anuzis well in that he has the positive traits associated with back slapping and the type of guy you'd like to have a beer with after a long day of organizing.

He also has an excellent understanding of campaign technology and the nuts and bolts of grassroots organizations. He has done work for Microsoft and other technology vendors who are on the cutting edge. He was also known as pushing the envelope of technology as Chairman of the Michigan Republican Party and encouraging other state parties across the country to participate in new media.

Anuzis has worked on presidential campaigns as a paid operative and served as Republican National Committeeman for Michigan. He was fairly close to being elected RNC Chairman on a couple of occasions and still has relationships across the country from those campaigns.

He is one of the few operatives who fundamentally understands the convention process and will be a key component of the Cruz operation at a contested convention.

The Rubio Campaign

The Rubio campaign was built from the ground up by establishment operatives from the world of Romney 2008. The campaign is probably the first in American history where the consultants stated openly what many consultants feel- that grassroots organizations essentially no longer require expensive offices and boots on the ground. The Rubio campaign received credit early on in the campaign for conserving resources, but this may become a liability in the stages of the campaign when state convention battles occur.

It remains to be seen which Rubio operatives are running the national convention delegate operations.

Rubio Campaign Manager: Terry Sullivan

Terry Sullivan is a very talented political operative who cut his teeth in the cutthroat world of South Carolina GOP politics. South Carolina has arguably the roughest, toughest, and most saturated GOP consultant community in the country. He was the South Carolina Director for Mitt Romney in 2008 and later served as Deputy Chief of Staff in Rubio's Senate office. He is partners with Warren Tompkins, another well-known South Carolina consultant. He earned a reputation on the 2016 Rubio campaign as a budget hawk. Supporters view his frugality as a badge of honor.

Senior Advisor: Todd Harris

Todd Harris is a founding partner at Something Else Strategies and was a senior strategist and media consultant on Rubio's 2010 campaign for U.S. Senate. He served as communications director on Fred Thompson's 2008 presidential campaign and was senior communications strategist for California Gov. Arnold Schwarzenegger. He is widely credited with Joni Ernst's successful 2014 bid for U.S. Senate in Iowa and the "make 'em squeal" ad.

The Bush Campaign

Any candidate with the last name Bush has a large reservoir of potential operatives from the Bush Tribe to choose from across the country. But like George W. Bush utilized Karl Rove to build a new organization that wasn't a mirror image of his father's organization, Jeb Bush similarly built an organization that was not a mirror image of his brother's organization. Instead he co-opted the establishment operatives of the national committees such as the NRSC in Washington, D.C. and combined them with some of his longtime Florida-based operatives.

Bush Consulting Firm: FP1

The political consulting firm with the most significant consolidation of establishment operatives in the country is FP1. Partners of FP1 fill the most significant staff and consulting positions in the Bush campaign. FP1 Partner Danny Diaz is the Campaign Manager. FP1 Partner Jon Downs is creating the TV ads for the Bush campaign. Trent Wisecup also previously worked for FP1 and currently serves as Director of Strategy for Bush's campaign.

Bush Advisor: Sally Bradshaw

Sally Bradshaw has long been considered the political operative closest to Jeb Bush and was previously an advisor to Governor Haley Barbour and his political action committee. She was a senior advisor on Mitt Romney's 2008 primary campaign but wasn't involved in the 2012 Romney campaign. She previously served as Chief of Staff for then-Governor Jeb Bush.

Bush Campaign Manager: Danny Diaz

Danny Diaz is an FP1 Partner and is known as one of the very best communications-based political operatives in the country today. He previously served as communications director for the Republican National Committee and deputy communications director for John McCain 2008. He replaced David Kochel as Campaign Manager in an early shakeup within the Bush campaign.

The Kasich Campaign

The Kasich campaign began with a 1-State Strategy and therefore built very little organization outside of New Hampshire in the early stages of the contest. However, they have very astute operatives on their team who understand what it will take to win a contested convention fight.

They are quickly building up their organization across the country and will likely gain assistance from supporters of other candidates such as Chris Christie as they drop from the race.

Kasich Campaign Manager: Beth Hansen

Beth Hanson was a Michigan Republican political operative until 1998 when she moved to Ohio to work for US Senator George Voinovich. She served as campaign manager for John Kasich's 2010 campaign and later served as his chief of staff. She is highly qualified and understands grassroots organization.

Senior Strategist: John Weaver

John Weaver is a tremendously experienced and talented political strategist with a storied history in American politics. He famously fought with Karl Rove before and after serving as Political Director for McCain's 2000 presidential campaign and strategist for McCain's 2008 campaign in the early days of the primary. He helped elect several senators and governors across the country and is widely recognized as one of the top strategists in the industry.

The Carson Campaign

The Carson campaign was one of the most effective small dollar fundraising campaigns in American history. They don't get enough credit for the juggernaut of millions of supporters across the country that they built.

Carson has never been elected to office before yet he raised more than any other Republican candidate in multiple fundraising quarters and for a short time was the leader in national polling.

Many candidates who have not run for office before make the mistake of listening to too many people and not letting the people in charge of the campaign run the campaign and make the final decisions. This was reportedly the case with the Carson and campaign. As a result, internal strife plagued the campaign at the end of 2015 and there was a significant shakeup in the campaign. The new campaign leaders are tremendously talented operatives with experience at several Republican National Conventions.

Carson Campaign Manager: Ed Brookover

Ed Brookover is a longtime GOP operative who has over 30 years of experience in campaign politics. He was Political Director of the NRCC from 1995-99 and National Field Director of the RNC during the 1986 cycle. He has experience in several Republican National Conventions and has a solid understanding of the process.

Carson Senior Communications Strategist: Jason Osborne

Jason Osborne is one of the most experienced national convention operatives in the country. He has worked at 6 out of the last 7 national conventions and literally was the founder oft he Black Hat program on the floor. He is also the Executive Director of the Northern Marianas Republican Party and has strong ties throughout the territories. Jason should be expected to find delegates where others cannot.

9. Republican National Committee

The Republican National Committee is a committee of 168 members with a Republican National Committeeman, Republican National Committeewoman, and State Chairman from each state, Washington, D.C., and the U.S. Territories for a total of 168 members.

RNC Leadership

Reince Priebus is the Chairman of the Republican National Committee and Sharon Day is the Co-Chairman.

The committee of 168 elects a Chairman, Co-Chairman, Secretary, and Treasurer every two years immediately following the November election, usually in January or February. Priebus is the longest serving RNC Chairman in history and is currently in his third and likely final term.

If Republicans win the White House, then the Republican President of the United States makes a recommendation for the committee of 168 to elect as their Chairman. These recommendations are historically approved, however, there has been pressure in recent years for the RNC Chairman to be a member of the Republican National Committee.

The 168

The 168 Members of the Republican National Committee meet twice per year for a Winter Meeting and a Summer Meeting.

They are Super Delegates to the National Convention, write many of the rules for the National Convention, and tend to be in positions of authority at the national convention. Therefore it is impossible to thoroughly understand the inner workings of the Republican National Convention without fundamentally understanding the history, personal relationships, and alliances on the Republican National Committee.

RNC Staff

The RNC Chairman hires operatives to manage a political department, finance department, communications department, digital department, member relations department, and any other staff they would like to hire.

Chief of Staff:	Katie Walsh
Chief Operating Officer:	Sean Cairncross
Chief Strategist:	Sean Spicer
Political Director:	Chris Carr
Finance Director:	Cara Mason
Director of Administration:	Robert Owens

Chairman Appointments

The RNC Chairman has the authority to appoint members of RNC committees, the Executive Committee, and the General Counsel.

The General Counsel is historically a very powerful position as a legal advisor to the Republican National Committee, and generally comes from the RNC membership. Previous General Counsels include David Norcross (who was a finalist to replace Haley Barbour as RNC Chairman), Mike Duncan, and Reince Priebus. The position is currently held by John Ryder from Tennessee.

There are also some key groups within the Republican National Committee Membership that are worth understanding. The most influential groups on the committee when it comes to electing the RNC Chairman are the Island Caucus and the Conservative Steering Committee.

Island Caucus

The recognized U.S. Territories include American Samoa, Guam, Northern Marianas, U.S. Virgin Islands, and Puerto Rico.

These islands formed a caucus decades ago in order to protect the rights of each other and to have a more significant impact in the election of the RNC Chairman by uniting the caucus as much as possible behind one candidate. They were critical in swinging the election to Michael Steele when Ken Blackwell dropped out of the race in the 2009 election for Chairman.

Holland Redfield, the Republican National Committeeman from the Virgin Islands, has served as the spokesperson for the island caucus in the past. He has drawn significant attention this primary season by encouraging RNC Chairman Reince Priebus and the rest of the Republican National Committee to more forcefully fight the candidacy of Donald Trump.

The caucus also includes Amata Radewagen, a Republican ex-officio member of the U.S. House of Representatives and the longest serving member of the RNC.

The islands are in a unique position to impact a contested national convention in Cleveland because some of them do not have a presidential preference poll and therefore the RNC Member super delegates and the national convention delegates who are elected will have significant autonomy on the convention floor.

It is in the realm of possibility that the Island Caucus unites to work together in the presidential and vice presidential selection process in much the same way they have worked together in RNC leadership elections.

Conservative Steering Committee

The Conservative Steering Committee (CSC) is the largest caucus within the RNC. Ninety-five of the 168 Members participate. The current Chairman of the CSC is Ellen Barrosse, the Republican National Committeewoman from Delaware. She succeeded Carolyn McLarty, the Republican National Committeewoman from Oklahoma.

History of RNC Chairman Elections

The role of an RNC Member on the national committee is often defined by their role in the election of the Chairman.

The seeds of the anti-establishment movement in the modern era were sewn in the election for Republican National Committee Chairman in 1997. Haley Barbour had run the Republican National Committee for four years and had been viewed as a very successful Chairman who took control of the House and Senate during the Republican Revolution of 1994.

But grassroots Republicans across the country were upset by what they viewed as a less than competent presidential campaign run by Bob Dole and his campaign team in 1996. The establishment-backed candidates for RNC Chairman were Governor Steve Merrill of New Hampshire and RNC General Counsel David Norcross. Social conservatives mostly from the south united behind Texas State Chairman Tom Pauken. There were two Midwestern candidates in Republican National Committeeman Chuck Yob from Michigan and Ohio State GOP Chairman Bob Bennett. Bennett dropped out after the first ballot and endorsed Yob but most of Bennett's delegates supported Nicholson instead. Chuck Yob and Tom Pauken then endorsed Jim Nicholson and he won.

Bob Dole had defeated Phil Gramm and other candidates for the Republican nomination. Nicholson and Yob were key supporters of the more conservative Gramm in the primary phase.

This turned control of the national Republican Party over to a new organization of conservatives who weren't favored by the GOP establishment.

ROUND	1	2	3	4	5	6
JIM NICHOLSON	23	30	38	65	74	winner
DAVID NORCROSS	41	46	47	50	47	withdrew
STEVE MERILL	42	42	43	46	43	withdrew
JOHN S. HERRINGTON	4	4	3	3	withdrew	
TOM PAUKEN	22	24	21	withdrew		
CHUCK YOB	17	18	12	withdrew		
BOB BENNETT	15	withdrew				

www.conventionchaos.com

The nature of the establishment is that most people assume when the chips are down the establishment will find a way to work together to maintain power and stop outsiders from winning. There was a critical moment in the 1997 RNC Chairman's election that questions this premise. The establishment candidates were Governor Steve Merrill of New Hampshire and RNC General Counsel David Norcross. Former George H.W. Bush White House Political Director and longtime Massachusetts Republican National Committeeman Ron Kaufman was representing Merrill. Kaufman and Norcross would meet and argue after every ballot about which candidate was going to drop out and endorse the other. Finally they couldn't agree, Norcross threw his arms up in the air, and they both ended up dropping out rather than work together – paving the way for Jim Nicholson to win.

The history of our party and of the Republican National Committee would be quite different if these two establishment operatives were able to come to agreement that day.

Bush 2000 Impact on the RNC

The election of George W. Bush in 2000 brought a new establishment to the country and he put his loyalists into key party positions. The first appointment as Chairman of the Republican National Committee was Governor Jim Gilmore of Virginia.

Governors were the political backbone of public support for Bush in the presidential primaries and he seemed determined to put his fellow Governors into positions of power. It proved awkward fairly quickly with the White House political operation run by Karl Rove and the Republican National Committee run by staff of Governor Jim Gilmore. The arrangement was short-lived and Montana Governor Marc Racicot was elected Chairman in 2002. In real terms, this was Karl Rove taking control of the RNC from the governors.

During the Bush Presidency there was a growing restlessness among RNC members. They were growing hungry for a Chairman who was truly chosen by the membership rather than appointed by the White House. Kentucky Republican National Committeeman Mike-Duncan, Treasurer and General Counsel of the RNC in 2001, was gradually groomed to be elected Chairman of the RNC in 2007 partly to minimize those concerns.

Barack Obama was elected President in 2008 and in 2009 there was anti-establishment energy sweeping the country. Mike Duncan was running for re-election but members did not want to keep the establishment in charge and wanted a new direction for the committee.

I was the Campaign Manager for Ken Blackwell and Blackwell dropped out after the fourth ballot to endorse Michael Steele. This essentially took the power of the RNC Chairmanship away from the establishment and led to the creation of a shadow Republican Party.

2007 CHAIRMAN ELECTION

ROUND	1	2	3	4	5	6
MICHAEL STEELE	46	48	51	60	79	91 winner
KATON DAWSON	28	29	34	62	69	77
SAUL ANUZIS	22	24	34	31	20	withdrew
KEN BLACKWELL	20	19	15	15	withdrew	
MIKE DUNCAN	52	48	44	withdrew		

www.conventionchaos.com

The Shadow Republican Party

After Michael Steele won the election, the Republican Party establishment put together multiple outsider groups related to American Crossroads. They very quickly became the boogeymen of the Tea Party and the face of the establishment, despite not controlling the RNC.

More importantly, this is a good demonstration of what the establishment will do when they lose control of the levers of power. Optimists would argue that they were doing what needed to be done in order to make sure the party maintained a well-funded operation to help elect Republicans up and down the ballot in 2010.

Skeptics would argue that they were siphoning money away from the Republican National Committee and setting the new RNC Chairman up for failure so that they could retake control of the party in 2011. Regardless of your perspective, history suggests that when the establishment loses control of the party, they will find a way to maintain their authority over the levers of power through other means.

10. Recent Convention History

The actions and reactions at State Conventions and the Republican National Conventions tend to define future conventions. There are a number of key things that happened over the past twenty years that are important to understand in the run up to the contested national convention in 2016.

1992 Buchanan Delegates

In some cases, there are fights over delegates even after there is a presumptive nominee. This occurred very prominently in 1992 when Buchanan wanted his delegates seated.

Chuck Yob was the Chairman of Contests at the 1992 Republican National Convention and was told by President George H.W. Bush to fight with Bay Buchanan over the Buchanan delegates for as long as possible to keep them busy and then at the end of the day give them everything they wanted so they are as happy as possible.

"The President told me to fight like hell all day long and then to do whatever Bay Buchanan asked for on the seating of delegates," said former Republican National Committeeman Chuck Yob of Michigan. It was clear that the Bush 1992 campaign wanted to use the contest fight as a distraction for the Buchanan team at the convention.

Stealing the McCain 2000 Michigan Delegates

A similar fight ensued in 2000 when McCain wanted his delegates seated in Michigan in compliance with the results of the Michigan primary. McCain won the Michigan primary by an overwhelming margin of 51% to 43% giving McCain 52 delegates and Bush only 6.

But when it came time to elect delegates to the National Convention, the Bush campaign decided they were going to steal those delegates and elect known and public Bush supporters as "McCain Delegates."

It was an unnecessary move that fanned the flames of division between McCain and Bush supporters and ultimately increased the erosion of clout once enjoyed by Governor John Engler's political organization. It is important to keep in mind that this happened only two years after the 1998 Attorney General race that was so decisive. It was yet another example of the establishment taking their power a step too far.

The Michigan delegates were the most public example of Supporters in Name Only, or SINOs. SINO is an acronym for delegates who disguise the candidate who they truly support in an effort to get elected National Convention Delegate.

2008 Lieberman Selection as Vice President

The fact is that Joe Lieberman was initially John McCain's preferred choice for vice president and arrangements were being made inside the McCain campaign to implement his selection.

When Mike DuHaime was brought in as Deputy Campaign Manager and Political Director in 2008, I was moved over to focus on the national convention in Minneapolis. The most important political project of the national convention was of course making sure that the vice presidential selection was approved by the convention delegates.

Lieberman campaigned for McCain in New Hampshire and was partly credited with helping McCain surge to victory over Mitt Romney in the New Hampshire primary. There was a belief within the McCain campaign, and quite possibly with McCain himself, that defeating the first African American nominee for president required something historic in nature. Therefore, choosing Lieberman was an obvious choice in some ways.

However, convincing a convention of grassroots conservatives from across the country to vote for a Democrat as their vice presidential nominee was going to be a significant task. The convention delegates were already distrustful of McCain from the fights between Bush and McCain, campaign finance reform, immigration, political flirtation with John Kerry, and other antagonistic political moves over the years.

I was tasked with putting together state convention teams to elect friendly delegates at state conventions across the country. We publicly said these teams were being put together to make sure that supporters of Ron Paul were not able to disrupt the national convention. This was partially true because there were several indications from Ron Paul supporters that they intended to shout at John McCain while he was giving his acceptance speech.

But the additional motive in expending staff and resources to the state conventions was to make sure that delegates were elected who would support McCain's choices in difficult decisions. Therefore, we scored every single delegate in the country to determine- on a scale of 1 to 5- whether each delegate would support Senator McCain's decisions on the convention floor regardless of whether they agreed with the decision. Conference calls were held with each and every state to go through and properly score the delegates. When I finally issued the report, it stated that roughly 70% of the delegates would support the decision, but that as many as 20% might walk out of the convention and cause a major public relations problem.

Ultimately, McCain went for a different type of historic choice with the selection of Alaska Governor Sarah Palin as the Republican vice presidential nominee.

Ron Paul Revolution 2008/12

There is perhaps nothing as important to the lead up oft he 2016 national convention as what happened with the Ron Paul campaigns in 2008 and 2012.

"You f$%$ers" screamed RNC counsel Ben Ginsberg to Ron and Rand Paul staff on the floor of the arena, in full earshot of delegates and press. "You f&$%ers are trying to nominate Ron from the floor and f#%! Up my convention. I will fix you f%$#ers for good."

Tampa 2012 was an intense scene, for no other reason than the Romney campaign and Republican National Committee decided to make it so. Delegates were threatened, screamed at, railroaded. Ron Paul staff were herded into hotel meeting rooms at 1am to get the same treatment. Rules were rewritten and rammed through- all to present to the world that there was only one name in nomination at the convention, and that that individual was the head of a unified party and convention. This was not so.

After being denied credentials to enter into the arena for two days, Ron and Rand Paul staff were doing their best to explain to the RNC that allowing Ron Paul to be nominated from the floor did them no harm, and in fact, would do some good. Romney easily had the delegates to win, and allowing, rather than stifling, a vote would ease the tensions and allow for goodwill and potentially some level of support for the nominee from those who attended as Paul supporters.

But the RNC and Romney campaign were having none of it. They were unseating delegates and credentialing slates that had not won. They also changed the number of state delegations needed to qualify for nomination from 5 to 8, all in the hopes of preventing a floor nomination.

Theoretically, they succeeded. Ron Paul was not nominated from the floor in Tampa. But did they really succeed? The culmination of a year of unnecessary vitriol and antagonism from the Romney/RNC brigade also succeeded in making sure Mitt Romney did not have the unified support of his party because a significant portion of the liberty and conservative movements felt shunned and mistreated.

Ron Paul certainly became the rallying point for the anti-establishment movement he began in 2007/8. The Tea Party movement sprung into full bloom after his campaign, watered by his campaign and the ensuing Campaign for Liberty launch, but also emulated by grassroots groups across America, rallying in opposition to debt, Obamacare, bailouts, and career politicians.

One such place was Bowling Green, Kentucky in 2009. Dr. Rand Paul, an eye surgeon, decided to stop by his local town square on April 15 to attend a Tea Party meeting.

Rand expected to see the normal few dozen people for a political meeting/rally in his small town and he told his wife Kelley he would stop by for a few minutes then come right home for dinner. When he arrived at the town square, there were 700 people gathered to hear speakers and to rally against Washington. It began the next phase of the revolution Ron Paul started and the Tea Party was continuing – getting like-minded outsiders like Rand to consider running for office themselves.

Rand's election was staffed, supported, and driven on the donations, work and expertise that came out of his father's campaign and Campaign for Liberty. When he decided to run against Mitch McConnell's hand-picked candidate, he knew he would have an uphill battle against a huge amount of money and influence – but he knew he wouldn't be alone.

In all, Rand was able to raise nearly dollar for dollar what his establishment opponent raised. He ran a great campaign on the issues and blew his opponent away by 24 points.

Others- like Mike Lee in Utah- accomplished similar feats, along with dozens of congressmen and state legislators. The anti-establishment, Tea Party, liberty wings of the party were flexing their muscle.
By 2011, Rand Paul had been in the U.S. Senate for just a few months, but was thrust into a role of supporting another bid for the presidency by his father.

The 2012 campaign would learn from the upstart 2008 operation. It would professionalize the top staff, and it would design and execute a full, all-out delegate hunting strategy, knowing it would be well funded. Ron Paul had raised over $40 million in 2008, but most of it was late and was a surprise, and structures were not always in place to take advantage. That would change for 2012.

Yet in state after state, the Paul operation found itself once again, even more so, fighting off the tricks, lies, rule changes – even the arrests – of the establishment desperate to keep them out of power in the party and at the national convention in Tampa.

The Paul operation had more success in 2012 than in 2008, including taking over county parties across the country and state parties in Iowa, Alaska, Maine, Nevada, and elsewhere.

The first voting of 2012 took place in Iowa on January 2, on a snowy night that ended up with more questions than answers.

The news media that night reported that the victor was narrowly Mitt Romney. Nearly a week later, they reported the victor was Rick Santorum.

By April, it turned out the winner that night was actually Ron Paul, which the Ron Paul campaign knew all along. One lesson for potential delegates and operatives was in play here: know the rules. In any political fight, if you don't know the rules, you might as well not play.

Political operatives from the Romney camp and others spent millions of dollars on TV, radio, mail, and web ads. They spent thousands of man hours knocking doors and making calls. They had large databases, sophisticated targeting, and impressive GOTV operations.

On caucus day, both Romney and Santorum performed, and performed at least as well as the Paul team, as Romney and Santorum finished a razor-thin first and second, with Paul a bit behind them in third. Then their people went home.

The Paul campaign however, made sure their very committed people stayed around for something else – the election of delegates to the county/state/national conventions that would take place from April to August.

Because the Paul caucus-goers were briefed, staffed, and ready, they carried the night, winning nearly 75 percent of the delegates, and taking over the entire Iowa state GOP, installing Ron Paul state chair A.J. Spiker as the new Iowa GOP chief after the previous chair resigned.

Ron Paul had already won a victory, one that would have an impact throughout the cycle and the country. But in other places, the results were not as clear. Reports of ballot stuffing, private vote tabulation, rigged rules and credentials were rampant throughout the process.

In Missouri, the convention started with the chairman breaking the rules by appointing, rather than electing, a convention chair and then, a la Nevada 2008, attempting to end the convention as he saw the Paul support winning the day. When Paul supporter Brent Stafford attempted to convene the convention outside in the parking lot, a swat team was called.

In Nevada, once again shenanigans continued- not the least of which was a special caucus held at the behest of one prominent donor. Paul supporters were literally turned away from it. The total fiasco that was the Nevada process led to the State Chair resigning immediately – and being replaced by leaders sympathetic to Paul including county chairs and the National Committeeman and Committeewoman.

In Maine, a circus ensued. The Maine caucuses don't take place on one day, they take place over a few weeks. The weekend before the last one, two counties (one of which was the only county won by Ron Paul in 2008) had their caucuses canceled due to a "snow emergency." Never mind that in 2008 the caucus was held with 8 inches of snow falling. Never mind that the "snow" never materialized. Ron Paul's strongest county was told it could hold a caucus later and be counted. This turned out to be a complete lie. In all, 3 of Maine's 16 counties had not voted when the state chair declared Mitt Romney the winner by less than 200 votes.

Ron Paul supporters continued on the process and won the majority of delegate slots, but ended up having their ranks cheated and unseated at the national convention in one of the nastier, unnecessary and underhanded moves of the whole cycle.

In Massachusetts, the home state of the presumptive nominee Romney, it was an utter embarrassment for Romney that turned into a railroading for Ron Paul supporters.

Paul supporters flooded the process, winning a majority of the delegates statewide. In one district, an 18-year-old high school student named Evan Kinney spoke with remarkable poise and eloquence asking to be a delegate. He followed the most recent statewide nominee of the party, Charlie Baker, the man who would go on to win the governor's mansion shortly thereafter.

Kinney won, beating Baker, former Lt. Governor Healey, and the House Minority leader for a delegate slot.

But the Massachusetts GOP wasn't done. They instituted a ridiculous oath committing the delegates under penalty of law and perjury to vote for Romney and had all pledged to do so. Delegates balked – what if something happened to Romney? They were bound by rules; they shouldn't be additionally bound by a flawed legal document.

In the confusion, the Massachusetts party simply decided to strip 17 Ron Paul delegates of their slots at the convention for failing to follow a new, legally questionable, rushed procedure that had no bearing on their duties.

To his credit, when Charlie Baker was informed of this and offered the delegate slot that had belonged to the 18-year-old Kinney, he refused to take it, noting he had lost fair and square in the party election. This was among the many reasons Baker, no libertarian, was able to count on the support of many Paul supporters in his next run. Fairness goes a long way- something the Romney camp would learn in reverse in a few short months.

The GOP convention in Tampa continued this tone and theme. Delegations were unseated. Rules were broken or changed. Delegates, staff, and politicians were threatened, overtly.

In a room at 1:00 a.m. one morning, when the Paul forces were still threatening to nominate Ron from the floor, high level RNC staff turned to Rand Paul staff in the room, and said "Well, if Ron Paul is nominated and speaks Monday, something will have to come off the schedule- perhaps a prime time speech that night that was previously scheduled." This was a not at all subtle reference to the speech Rand Paul was set to give that night- 15 minutes in prime time.

Doug Stafford, Rand's Chief Strategist, turned to the RNC staff and declared, "Rand Paul is giving a speech at 8:00 p.m. Monday night. Whether he gives it inside the building with your microphone or outside it with mine is entirely up to you." Attempts to quell the situation were futile.

Paul delegates accomplished much in 2012. They won party organizations. They learned the rules and used them for platforms and leadership. They sent a mass of new delegates to a convention they could not win, hoping to be brought in as part of a new wing of the party, ready to give it energy and direction. They left embittered and determined to keep fighting against, rather than join, the questionable party that turned them away.

2012 Dele-GATE

Mitt Romney narrowly defeated Rick Santorum in the Michigan primary 41% to 38%. Michigan only had 30 delegates and they were almost all awarded in congressional districts. So each of the 14 districts received 2 delegates each, and then there were 2 statewide delegates. Santorum and Romney each won 7 congressional districts so they each received 14 district delegates. This left the two At-Large Delegates to be divided up.

The rules clearly stated that they should be divided proportionally and therefore each candidate would receive one At-Large Delegate. But the Romney campaign threw a fit and convinced the credentials committee of the Michigan Republican Party to cheat and award both delegates to Romney in violation of the rules.

This led to a massive controversy in the Michigan Republican Party. We immediately canvassed the state with telephone calls identifying people who were upset by the cheating and found hundreds of new people to storm the state convention who were upset with the actions of the establishment.

Saul Anuzis was the Republican National Committeeman and therefore had a vote on the credentials committee. He was a loyal supporter of Mitt Romney and voted with the Romney campaign's wishes on the credentials committee, and ultimately defended the move publicly.

He deserves credit for taking one for the team. The vote cost Anuzis his position on the Republican National Committee with Dave Agema defeating him in a blowout on the convention floor. The establishment had not learned their lesson from the 2010 state convention.

11. 2016 Republican National Convention

The Republican National Convention is the supreme authority of the Republican Party and can essentially do whatever it wants as it relates to all matters of the Republican Party including the presidential and vice presidential nominations.

The Republican National Convention will be held in Cleveland, Ohio from July 18-21, 2016 and is organized by a committee appointed by RNC Chairman Reince Priebus called the Committee on Arrangements (COA).

Committee on Arrangements (COA)

The Republican National Committee Chairman appoints one RNC Member from every state and territory to serve on the Committee on Arrangements (COA). The Committee on Arrangements (COA) officially determines important matters such as hotel assignments, floor seating, and other critical matters. In practice, the COA historically has waited until the presumptive nominee is selected by voters so that the nominee-in-waiting's campaign can put their stamp on the logistics of the convention.

The RNC Chairman also appoints the COA Chairman and COA Co-Chairman to run the COA.

Convention Chairman Steve King

RNC Chairman Reince Priebus appointed longtime ally Steve King as Chairman of the COA. King has been the RNC National Committeeman from Wisconsin since 2007 and ran for United States Senate in 1988.

Convention Co-Chairman Joanne Davidson

RNC Chairman Reince Priebus appointed former RNC Co-Chairman Joanne Davidson as the Co-Chairman of the COA. Davidson has been National Committeewoman from Ohio since 2004. Davidson was Chairman of the Committee on Arrangements for the 2008 National Convention.

The Committee on Arrangements was announced by Chairman Reince Priebus on April 23, 2015 and includes:

Vicki Drummond, National Committeewoman, Alabama
Ralph Seekins, National Committeeman, Alaska
Amata Radewagen, National Committeewoman, American Samoa
Sharon Giese, National Committeewoman, Arizona
Jonathan Barnett, National Committeeman, Arkansas
Linda Ackerman, National Committeewoman, California
Lilly Nuñez, National Committeewoman, Colorado
John Frey, National Committeeman, Connecticut
Laird Stabler, National Committeeman, Delaware
Jill Homan, National Committeewoman, District of Columbia
Blaise Ingoglia, State Chairman, Florida
Linda Herren, National Committeewoman, Georgia
Margaret Metcalfe, National Committeewoman, Guam
Miriam Hellreich, National Committeewoman, Hawaii
Damond Watkins, National Committeeman, Idaho
Demetra DeMonte, National Committeewoman, Illinois
John Hammond, National Committeeman, Indiana
Steve Scheffler, National Committeeman, Iowa
Kelly Arnold, State Chairman, Kansas
Steve Robertson, State Chairman, Kentucky
Ross Little, National Committeeman, Louisiana
Alex Willette, National Committeeman, Maine
Louis Pope, National Committeeman, Maryland
Ron Kaufman, National Committeeman, Massachusetts

Ronna Romney McDaniel, State Chairwoman, Michigan
Janet Beihoffer, National Committeewoman, Minnesota
Jeanne Luckey, National Committeewoman, Mississippi
Lance Beshore, National Committeeman, Missouri
Betti Hill, National Committeewoman, Montana
Joyce Simmons, National Committeewoman, Nebraska
Michael McDonald, State Chairman, Nevada
Steve Duprey, National Committeeman, New Hampshire
Bill Palatucci, National Committeeman, New Jersey
Rosie Tripp, National Committeewoman, New Mexico
Ed Cox, State Chairman, New York
David Lewis, National Committeeman, North Carolina
Sandy Boehler, National Committeewoman, North Dakota
James Ada, State Chairman, Northern Mariana Islands
Jim Dicke, National Committeeman, Ohio
Matt Borges, State Chairman, Ohio
Steve Fair, National Committeeman, Oklahoma
Donna Cain, National Committeewoman, Oregon
Christine Toretti, National Committeewoman, Pennsylvania
Zori Fonalledas, National Committeewoman, Puerto Rico
Lee Ann Sennick, National Committeewoman, Rhode Island
Cindy Costa, National Committeewoman, South Carolina
Dana Randall, National Committeeman, South Dakota
Peggy Lambert, National Committeewoman, Tennessee
Toni Anne Dashiell, National Committeewoman, Texas
Bruce Hough, National Committeeman, Utah
Jay Shepard, National Committeeman, Vermont
Lilliana Belardo de O'Neal, National Committeewoman, Virgin Islands
Kathy Hayden, National Committeewoman, Virginia
Fredi Simpson, National Committeewoman, Washington
Kris Warner, National Committeeman, West Virginia
Mary Buestrin, National Committeewoman, Wisconsin
Greg Schaefer, National Committeeman, Wyoming

Chairman Reince Priebus also appointed a Republican National Convention Staff made up of several people who have been involved in the RNC and past national conventions.

Convention CEO: Jeff Larson

Jeff Larson is a well-known and highly respected political consultant who has served as Senior Advisor to the Republican National Committee, CEO to the 2008 National Convention in Minneapolis, and ran the Independent Expenditure arm for the NRSC in 2014.

Laron formed Feather Hodges Larson & Synhorst in 1999, which became FLS-DCI and then FLS Connect, a GOP consulting firm that specializes in telephone calls and other technologies.

He was appointed convention CEO of the 2016 by Chairman Priebus, a role that he held previously.

He is in a difficult position because there are plenty of skeptics leery of the role FLS has played with the RNC in recent years, and there will be concerns of favoritism for FLS partners that work on competing presidential campaigns.

Regardless, Larson is a smart and capable operative who is well qualified to run the national convention.

Director of Community and Political Affairs: Chris McNulty

Chris McNulty served as Political Director of the Ohio Republican Party in the successful 2000 Election Cycle, Executive Director of the Ohio Republican Party from 2001to 2006, RNC Midwest Regional Political Director from 2006-2010 and RNC Political Director from 2013 to 2015. He was credited with running a very competent state party organization under the leadership of the late Chairman Bob Bennett.

Differences from Past Conventions

The 2016 Republican National Convention will be contested and is therefore substantially different from previous conventions that began with a presumptive nominee. For example:

1) Control of Convention - Convention staff and Committee on Arrangements members will have far greater authority in this convention relative to previous conventions because there won't be a presumptive nominee with campaign staff taking over the political management of the national convention.

2) Messaging - There will be less candidate-specific messaging than normal because there won't be a presumptive nominee to organize the candidate-specific messaging for the general election.

3) The election of members to the Rules Committee, Platform Committee, and other committees of the convention become even more important because they could be determinative in laying the foundation for the election of the Republican nominee for president and vice president.

Control of Convention

There is usually a presumptive nominee for president established through the primary process by April of the election year. The presumptive nominee gains control of the levers of power of the Republican National Convention in April or May of the election year. Therefore, the real positions of authority within the convention infrastructure change dramatically and the convention staff essentially become auxiliaries of the presidential campaign.

There are legal separations and therefore there isn't necessarily direct ordering of staff, but at the end of the day the presumptive nominee ends up getting what they want on any given decision, and puts many loyal people into positions of power up and down the convention management organization.

A contested convention means the convention staff and the Committee on Arrangements (COA) of the Republican National Committee will have more authority than usually in the running of the convention.

Messaging

The Republican National Committee, convention staff, and COA will have tough decisions to make in terms of what to emphasize at the convention from a messaging perspective. The process of a convention is not an attractive thing for voters at home to watch play out on TV and in many cases the process can be downright disgusting.

There won't be a presumptive nominee to organize the messaging around so they will likely come up with a set of principles to highlight, and emphasize the contrasts with the leaders of the opposing party.

Election of Convention Committees

There is a critically important election that happens within each national convention state delegation soon after the selection of national convention delegates. Every delegation will elect a delegation chairman and two delegates to sit on each of the following committees: Rules and Order of Business, Credentials, Platform, and Permanent Organization.

The presidential campaigns need to aggressively participate in both the election of national convention delegates and the election of convention committee members from the delegations to make sure their voice is heard on these very important committees.

For example, rules can be changed or clarified to impact critical matters such as ballot access for the candidates, the binding of delegates from ballot to ballot, the selection of the vice president, and other critical matters.

12. Rules

The most important aspect of any national convention is the rules. Once the convention convenes, the convention controls all aspects of the nomination process for president and vice president. The RNC Chairman, officers, members, campaigns, lawyers, donors, and even the courts are powerless in the face of a majority and/or supermajority of the delegates to the national convention. The rules that govern the activities of the delegates are critical.

Rules Meant to Apply from Convention to Convention

The Republican National Convention previously ruled from convention to convention. This meant that the rules for one convention were set for the next convention, and could not be changed between conventions. This was a very good policy that minimized the opportunity for political operatives to adjust the rules to benefit their campaign - or hurt an opposing campaign - in the middle of the cycle.

Unfortunately, the Republican National Convention essentially voted at the 2012 convention that they were going to allow the Republican National Committee to vote to set the initial rules for the 2016 convention at an RNC meeting after the 2012 elections. This lead to a number of rules changes that were put forward to hurt candidates with support from a minority of the delegates and help candidates who were perceived as the frontrunners for the nomination.

Timing of Rules

It is important to note that rules aren't approved for the 2016 convention until the 2016 convention begins. Any discussion of what the current convention rules are is simply a discussion of the starting place of the rules that will begin the discussion at the convention Rules Committee, and then ultimately be approved or amended from the floor of the convention.

The Old Dirty Secret - Lack of Binding

The dirty secret of presidential primary politics prior to the 2016 convention was that most of the primaries don't matter, or at least not in real terms. The only reason New Hampshire and other early states mattered was because they provided financial and earned media momentum that could potentially lead to victories in other states and the sense of inevitability.

For example, John McCain won New Hampshire in 2008 and received a disproportionate amount of mainstream media attention as a result of that victory. This led to increased favorables in other states whose primaries followed New Hampshire. And most importantly, it led to a dramatic increase in fundraising.

In real terms, however, a presidential candidate is nominated based on receiving a majority of the votes of the delegates to the national convention.

But there were very few states – if any – who had to bind their delegations to the result of the primary. And there was even some question as to whether the state rules that mandated binding even applied at the national convention, or whether they could be enforced.

Binding

The most considerable change to the 2016 RNC Convention rules mandated that delegates were bound on the first ballot to vote in accordance with delegate allocation rules as passed by their state committees and approved by the Republican National Committee.

This was arguably first implemented with a small change of wording at the

2008 convention, and included again in the initial rules for the 2016 convention.

The most interesting aspect of the current binding rule, however, is that it does not address the circumstances under which a delegate becomes unbound. In other words, if the rules are strictly followed, and not changed, then if no candidate receives a majority on the first ballot, then we would never have a nominee.

(a) Binding and Allocation.

(1) Any statewide presidential preference vote that permits a choice among candidates for the Republican nomination for President of the United States in a primary, caucuses, or a state convention must be used to allocate and bind the state's delegation to the national convention in either a proportional or winner-take-all manner, except for delegates and alternate delegates who appear on a ballot in a statewide election and are elected directly by primary voters.

The convention rules have a section that addresses the power of states to address matters that are not addressed by the national convention rules. For example, the national convention rules state that all delegates must be bound on the results of the presidential preference vote. But they do not address what happens to delegates who are bound to a candidate who either drops out of the race, suspends their campaign, or is not nominated as a result of falling short of the threshold under Rule 40(b).

This determination seems reserved for the states.

But this still raises the question: if the national rules trump state rules, and if the national rules say delegates are bound, and don't say that there is a limitation to that binding, then how would state rules ever be able to unbind their delegates?

Ballot Access - Rule 40

The most controversial of the rules changes was what is known as Rule 40. Rule 40(b) changed the rules for ballot access to make it much more difficult for a candidate to receive ballot access at the Republican National Convention.

The passing of Rule 40 almost assures that the Republican National Convention in Cleveland will be chaos as candidates who do not have a majority of eight states fight to change the rules at the last minute and gain ballot access at the convention.

Winner-Take-All

The other critical change to the rules applies to when a state can have their primary or caucus without RNC penalty. The changes made it so that:

1. Only the 4 "carve out" states of Iowa, New Hampshire, South Carolina, and Nevada states could go before March 1st without a penalty.

2. Any state that goes between March 1st and March 14th must be proportional in some method - although there is significant flexibility in how the proportion is calculated relative to statewide, partially by congressional district, thresholds to earn delegates, etc.

3. Any state that goes after March 14th can go winner-take-all if they choose, but they do not have to and most did not.

The RNC had the authority to put forward these rules and guidelines, but ultimately it is up to the state Republican parties, legislatures, and governors to implement the delegate allocation procedures for their respective state.

The reality is that some states can change their nomination contest rules and primary dates easier than other states. In some cases, the State GOP Chairman can essentially implement their will at the state committee and legislative levels, in other cases the elected officials work together to accomplish something that they perceive to be good for their state. But in many cases changes are too difficult to make in the context of other local political fights and conflicting priorities. For example, asking a Democrat Governor and a Democrat state legislature to take action to help the Republican Party is often a fool's errand at best.

As a result, only nine states representing 391 delegates, or 15.8% of the overall convention delegate total, are chosen from states using "winner-take-all."

All other states are proportional in some manner, and therefore most of them - especially the earlier states - will make it difficult or impossible for any candidate to achieve a majority within a state delegation. Again ballot access requires a majority – not a plurality – of the delegates from eight states. That is a very high threshold to meet in a multi-candidate field.

This dramatically limits the number of states that a candidate can use as their ballot access states because very few states will give any candidate a majority of their delegates.

Rules TBD

There has been plenty of discussion in the media of problematic rules pertaining to ballot access. But the real controversy in the lead-up to the national convention will be related to the binding of delegates.

There will be some, such as Republican National Committeeman Curly Haugland, who argue that binding doesn't exist. But let us assume for the purposes of this book that binding does exist.

If the current rules are followed, then it would be very difficult for any candidate to ever get to a majority. It would need to be built solely upon the delegates they earned through the primary process, and the six delegations (American Samoa, Colorado, Guam, North Dakota, Virgin Islands, Wyoming) that are unbound. This is because there is no mechanism within the party rules for unbinding delegates, and there is no limit articulated in the rule for the binding of delegates.

The rules never say that the rules only bind delegates for the first ballot and they don't say that delegates assigned to a particular candidate are unbound if that candidate suspends or drops out of the campaign.

Therefore, the Convention Committee on Rules and Order of Business will likely address and clarify the issue of binding in their report, and ultimately all national convention delegates will have the opportunity to vote on or amend that report.

It is possible that the committee, and ultimately the convention, will decide to only bind delegates for the first ballot. Alternatively they could bind for all ballots except in cases where a candidate drops out or suspends their campaign, or they could eliminate binding completely and throw the convention into further chaos. Some questions to think about:

- Does binding even currently exist?

- If a candidate doesn't have a majority after the 1st ballot, how would they ever get to a majority if the binding rules aren't adjusted to release after the 1st ballot?

- What happens to bound delegates after the first ballot?

- What happens to delegates who are bound to a candidate who suspends their campaign, or fails to get a majority of eight states to get on the ballot?

The   rules   are   unclear.

Changing the Rules…..Again…

The rules need to be updated and clarified by the convention committee on rules as well as the convention as a whole.

But this puts both the establishment in a difficult position. It is always dangerous for the establishment to attempt to change the rules partway through the contest. Some will even call it cheating.

There are some things that need to be determined and clarified. But they could easily take it a step too far. There have been media reports that some within the establishment are threatening to change the rules if one of their preferred candidates does not achieve ballot access legitimately.

The logistical problem the establishment will face when trying to change the rules is that the Rules Committee will be elected by the state delegations rather than appointed by the RNC Chairman. This will mean that the committee is largely loyal to the respective campaign the delegate supports rather than the National Chairman of the Republican Party.

Will state delegations really vote to elect rules committee members who will do the establishment's bidding to allow their preferred candidate ballot access, or change the binding rules to help them? Doubtful.

But even if the establishment is successful, playing games with the rules has serious ramifications that could turn a convention into total chaos, or even a catastrophe. Who decides what is necessary, and what is a step too far?

13. Contests

The most controversial fights at recent Republicans National Conventions are contests in the seating of delegates. There is often disagreement within a state as to who should be the duly elected delegates from that state. For example, if one faction in a state believes rules were broken, or that someone wasn't a supporter of a particular presidential candidate, or deadlines weren't met.

These fights are usually largely formalities in that there aren't hotly contested fights that will ultimately impact the final result of the presidential or vice presidential nominations. They are always very important to the people trying to be seated, and the states impacted, but ultimately they usually are not determinative of anything substantive.

However, this convention is likely to have several matters such as ballot access, presidential nomination votes, and vice presidential nomination votes that could be decided by a small number of delegates. For example, a single delegate could easily swing whether or not a candidate has a majority of a state that is one of their eight states for ballot access.

Rules 21-25 outline the procedures that are in place to deal with challenges to a delegate's credentials:

Rule Number 21
- Contests for District Delegates elected by District Conventions are decided by its state convention or state committee unless the contest

arises out of irregular or unlawful action by the state committee or state convention. In that case the Republican National Committee can take jurisdiction.

- Contests for At-Large Delegates are presented to the Republican National Committee.

Rule Number 22

- Delegates who are being contested cannot vote until their contest is settled. They can be given the right to vote on matters other than their contest by an affirmative vote of a majority of the Republican National Committee or the Convention Committee on Credentials.

Rule Number 23

- Contests need to be filed no later than 30 days before the national convention.
- Contests must be filed by a resident of the relevant state.

Rule Number 24

- The Standing Committee on Contests shall promptly hear contests, decide its recommendation, and submit its recommendation for resolution by the Republican National Committee.
- The Republican National Committee will make a determination on the recommendation.

Rule Number 25

- Determinations made by the Republican National Committee can be appealed to the Convention Committee on Credentials.
- No contests can originate before the Convention Committee on Credentials. They must originate before the Standing Committee on Contests.

14. Delegates

There are 2,472 total delegates to the Republican National Convention. Therefore, 1,237 delegates are required to win the Republican nomination for President of the United States. These numbers could change slightly based on the credentialing process at the convention if there are challenges to various delegations.

The delegates to the national convention run the convention themselves and every delegate has only one vote. All delegates are equal with the exception of being governed by rules such as binding. There is no one who can overrule the will of the delegates. There is no unit rule voting.

The delegates are distributed to the delegations as follows:

- 10 At-Large Delegates from each of the 50 states
- The State Chairman, National Committeeman, and National committeewoman from each state and American Samoa, Washington, D.C., Guam, Northern Mariana Islands, Puerto Rico, and the Virgin Islands
- 3 Delegates for each Representative in the U.S. House of Representatives from each state
- 6 Delegates At-Large from American Samoa, Guam, Northern Marianas Islands, and U.S. Virgin Islands
- 16 Delegates At-Large from Washington, D.C.
- 20 Delegates At-Large from Puerto Rico

- Each state who casted its electoral votes for the Republican nominee for President of the United States in the last election receives 4.5 Delegates At-Large plus a number of the Delegates At-Large equal to 60% of the number of electoral votes of that state
- 1 Delegate At-Large for a Republican Governor
- 1 Delegate At-Large if Republicans have at least 50% of that state's congressional delegation
- 1 Delegate At-Large for having a majority of a state legislative chamber
- 1 Delegate At-Large for having a majority of all state legislative chambers within the state
- 1 Delegate At-Large for every U.S. Senator within the state.

There are three types of delegates: At-Large (AL), Congressional District (CD), and Republican National Committee Members (RNC).

At-Large: Delegates who are selected by a statewide vote are referred to as At-Large delegates. Every state received 10 At-Large delegates, and also receive additional At-Large delegates based on whether the state has a Republican Governor, Republican U.S. Senator, State Legislative control, etc. Territories receive 6 At-Large delegates rather than 10.

Congressional District (CD): Every state is allocated 3 delegates per congressional district and the delegates must be residents of the CD they represent.

Republican National Committee Members (RNC Members): The 3 RNC Members from each state, territory, and Washington, D.C. are automatic delegates to the national convention. They are bound to the statewide winner on the first ballot according to the initially proposed rules.

Alternates

There is also an alternate elected for every delegate with the exception of the RNC Members. There are no alternates for RNC Members.

Delegate Allocations

States and territories needed to submit their delegate allocation rules in final format to the Republican National Committee by October 1, 2015. The only delegation that did not properly submit their allocation method on time was the Virgin Islands, and therefore they had to revert back to the rules that were utilized in 2012.

There are essentially four methods of delegate allocations that were submitted by the states and territories: Proportional, Winner-take-all, Hybrid, and Unbound.

Proportional: The proportional method means that the delegates are allocated in proportion to the presidential preference poll that is taken at the presidential primary or caucus. All states that have their preference poll between March 1st and March 14th must be proportional. There are two ways of going proportional. Delegations can either be proportional statewide or proportional both statewide and within congressional districts. There is also an exception that some states that go proportional can still allocate their delegates winner-take-all if a candidate receives over 50% of the vote.

Winner-take-all: Winner-take-all means that a candidate received all the delegates from the state or territory in return for winning a plurality of the presidential preference vote.

Hybrid: Hybrid models combine various methods of proportional and winner-take-all. Hybrid models are permitted after March 14th.

Unbound: States and territories that are unbound don't have a presidential preference vote.

15. State Order and Distribution

The importance of states to the presidential nominating process has for decades been perceived to be based on the order of placement on the nomination calendar. This is largely a function of the post-1950's conventions that were driven more by media and momentum than by backroom deals among party bosses.

Before media momentum between primaries became so influential in the nominating process, the larger delegations were viewed to be more important regardless of their place on the calendar. This was because there was no binding of delegates at the national level and therefore the state delegations were often not representative of the will of the voters in that particular state.

There will be many factors that contribute to the importance of a state in 2016. The timing of the contest, the size of the delegation, the manner that the delegates are apportioned, and what freedom the delegation has within their state and national rules.

Here is the official order of states as released by the Republican National Committee:

Delegates to the 2016 Republican National Convention
Arranged by Month, Date, and State

Summary

There are 2,472 delegates to the 2016 Republican National Convention. Therefore, 1,237 delegates are currently required to secure the Republican nomination for President of the United States outright.

February — **133 Delegates**

Date			State
1st	(30 / 30)	(1% / 1%):	Iowa (30)
9th	(23 / 53)	(1% / 2%):	New Hampshire (23)
20th	(50 / 103)	(2% / 4%):	South Carolina (50)
23rd	(30 / 133)	(1% / 6%):	Nevada (30)

March — **1,434 Delegates**

Date			State
1st	(595/ 728)	(24% / 29%):	Alabama (50), Alaska (28), Arkansas (40), Georgia (76), Massachusetts (42), Minnesota (38), Oklahoma (43), Tennessee (58), Texas (155), Vermont (16), Virginia (49)
5th	(155/ 883)	(6% / 36%):	Kansas (40), Kentucky (46), Louisiana (46), Maine (23)
6th	(23 / 906)	(1% / 37%):	Puerto Rico (23)
8th	(150 / 1,056)	(6% / 43%):	Hawaii (19), Idaho (32), Michigan (59), Mississippi (40)
10th	(9 / 1,065)	(.4% / 43%)	U.S. Virgin Islands (9)
12th	(28 / 1,093)	(1% / 44%):	District of Columbia (19), Guam (9)
15th	(367 / 1,460)	(15% / 59%):	Florida (99), Illinois (69), Missouri (52), North Carolina (72), Northern Marianas (9), Ohio (66)
22nd	(107 / 1,567)	(4% / 64%):	American Samoa (9), Arizona (58), Utah (40)

April — **403 Delegates**

Date			State
1st	(28 / 1,595)	(1% / 65%)	North Dakota (28)
5th	(42 / 1,637)	(2% / 66%):	Wisconsin (42)
9th	(37 / 1,674)	(1% / 68%)	Colorado (37)
16th	(29 / 1,703)	(1% / 69%)	Wyoming (29)
19th	(95 / 1,798)	(4% / 73%):	New York (95)
26th	(172 / 1,970)	(7% / 80%):	Connecticut (28), Delaware (16), Maryland (38), Pennsylvania (71), Rhode Island (19)

May — **199 Delegates**

Date			State
3rd	(57 / 2,027)	(2% / 82%):	Indiana (57)
10th	(70 / 2,097)	(3% / 85%):	Nebraska (36), West Virginia (34)
17th	(28 / 2,125)	(1% / 86%):	Oregon (28)
24th	(44 / 2,169)	(2% / 88%):	Washington (44)

June — **303 Delegates**

Date			State
7th	(303 / 2,472)	(12% / 100%):	California (172), Montana (27), New Jersey (51), New Mexico (24), South Dakota (29)

*official document from the RNC

Performing well in the early states of Iowa, New Hampshire, South Carolina, and Nevada provide momentum going into March 1 and March 15 when a significant number of states hold their contests.

Iowa serves its normal role in winnowing the field down, New Hampshire provides a jolt of momentum, South Carolina crowns a front runner, and the March states will determine whether there is a presumptive nominee or not.

The new rule requiring states that go prior to March 15th to distribute their delegations proportionally (exclusive of early carve out states) extended the nomination calendar and made it less likely that a candidate will receive a majority of the delegates prior to the national convention.

Size of the Delegation

Delegations from large states such as California, Texas, New York, and Florida have outsized influence, but it doesn't only matter how big the delegation is, it also matters significantly how the delegates are distributed within each respective state.

Delegate Distribution Within States

There are other important attributes of the state delegations other than simply the date of the presidential primary or caucus. For example, winner-take-all states are more important than proportional states because candidates win far more delegates by winning a plurality of the vote, but they are also at risk of having fake supporters that we refer to as SINOs (Supporters in Name Only).

The media often says that states that are on March 15th or after are winner-take-all. That is not technically correct. States that are March 15th or after are allowed to go winner-take-all, but most of them did not utilize that option for delegate distribution and instead maintained their past rules as a proportional state.

Here are the official classification counts by the Republican National Committee:

	# STATES	# DELEGATES	PERCENTAGE
PROPORTIONAL*	31	1,347	54.5%
WINNER-TAKE-ALL	9	391	15.8%
HYBRID	10	613	24.8%
NO PREFERENCE VOTE	6	121	4.9%

* The majority of proportional states have thresholds of 15% or more

TOTAL DELEGATES: 2,472

	# DELEGATES	SINGLE MONTH PERCENTAGE	CUMULATIVE PERCENTAGE
FEBRUARY	133	6%	6%
MARCH	1,434	58%	64%
APRIL	403	16%	80%
MAY	199	8%	88%
JUNE	303	12%	100%

official document from the RNC

The vast majority of states (31) are distributing their delegates in some type of proportional method. This rarely means, however, that it is strictly proportional in that the percentage that a candidate wins in the primary will equal the percentage of delegates they receive. There are usually several other variables in the calculation such as having to hit a threshold of 10% or 15% of the vote in order to receive any delegates.

Regardless of the proportional system utilized, in any state with a nominating contest before March 15- and in most states with a contest after that date- unless a candidate wins a majority of the votes from a state, they will receive less than half of their delegates. This means that very few, if any, of the states that go before March 15th could be used as one of a candidate's eight states to achieve ballot access at the national convention.

This does not only impact ballot access, it also severely limits the potential for a presumptive nominee to ever emerge. Even if a candidate won every single state they would still not have a majority of the delegates until late April or early May because far more states go proportional rather than winner-take-all and some of the biggest winner-take-all states such as New Jersey are very late in the process.

16. SINOs

The most important concept at play in 2016 is the likely surge in the number of people who are bound by rules to vote for a candidate at the national convention that they don't truly support. CHAOS coins the name Supporters in Name Only (SINOs) to define these people.

SINOs have been around for a long time but they previously didn't live in the shadows. The 2000 Michigan delegates, for example, didn't hide the fact that they didn't support John McCain. The Bush people stole them, and they were proud of it.

The RNC passed a rule binding the delegates to the results of the preference poll. These rules still need to be approved by the convention Rules Committee and the convention as a whole. Assuming they are approved, there will be a number of delegates who are elected across the country who don't actually support the candidate that they are bound to support on the ballot.

This has tremendous ramifications for the election of the important committees such as the Rules Committee that will ultimately make, amend, or approve the rules – including those rules related to the binding of delegates.

For example, the first thing a delegation will do after being elected in each respective state will be to elect convention committee members. If delegates from Michigan are allocated to Trump based on the result of the primary, but people who are more favorable towards Cruz are elected at the state convention, then it is likely that Cruz people will fill the convention committee slots from Michigan rather than Trump people.

This will dramatically impact procedural matters from the floor. For example, if there is a vote to eliminate binding from the floor of the convention, and the Trump campaign opposes it, but the Cruz campaign supports it, then those same delegates will likely vote with the Cruz campaign again even though they are technically allocated to the Trump campaign.

This could happen over an over again.

The most problematic action of these SINO's would be for them to use their position to swing momentum on the ballot that follows the lifting of binding. The first ballot that allows delegates to vote their true hearts and minds is going to have a far different result than the last ballot that binds the delegates based on the result of the primary or caucus.

When the election goes multiple ballots, there will be a large number of swing delegates and those delegates will be watching for momentum to make sure that they are on the winning side.

These momentum swings will likely be determinative in selecting the presidential nominee.

For these reasons SINO's are critical to watch in the committee elections in the lead up to the convention as well as on the convention floor in the presidential nomination vote.

17. Delegate Selection

How are each respective states' delegates elected and what does that say about their motives on the convention floor?

Most analysis of state delegations at a national convention is based on the date of each state's primary or caucus, the size of the delegation, or the power of the individuals within a delegation. But this does not say anything about the number of SINOs in a delegation, the motives of a delegation, or the freedom of the delegation to make deals on the floor.

The system that is used to elect national convention delegates in each state becomes a dominant variable in a contested convention and are window to see which candidates over perform at a national convention relative to their performance in the primaries.

This book is the first to classify the delegations on the basis of how their delegates were elected. The states can be broken up into four segments in terms of importance to the nomination at the Republican National Convention:

1. **Early States -** The early states are always going to be very important because of their placement on the calendar. From a strict delegate perspective, South Carolina is the most important of the early states because it is the only state that uses a modified Winner-take-all methodology. Regardless, we classify early states as their own segment because of their importance on the calendar.

2. **Free Agents** - The states and territories that have delegates who are not committed to any particular presidential nominee are by far the most important delegations to a contested 2016 Republican National Convention, especially in the early stages such as committee assignments, ballot access, and early ballots. In some cases- such as North Dakota- all the delegates are likely to be free agents. In others like the Virgin Islands, some of the delegates could be unaffiliated and some could be bound as a result of their stated preference on their delegate filing application.

3. **State Conventions** - The states and territories that elect their delegates through a state convention process are the next most important delegations to the Republican National Convention. These delegations will be less loyal to the campaign that they are bound to vote for because they are largely individually elected, and not necessarily supporters of the candidate that they are bound to vote for by rule. There will be many SINO's in state convention states.

4. **Balloted** - The states and territories that elect their delegates directly on the ballot will have the least amount of freedom on the convention floor because they were generally asked to be put on the ballot by the presidential campaign that won their state or congressional district. Therefore, convention delegates from balloted states will be the most loyal delegates on the convention floor and therefore aren't as important in terms of swinging votes. Included in this category are states such as California that allow the campaigns to select the delegates. There will be few SINO's in balloted states.

The Early States: Iowa

Iowa is a critical state in winnowing the field and possibly giving candidates who over perform some degree of momentum heading into New Hampshire and South Carolina.

But Iowa is historically a state that also allowed the opportunity for candidates to steal delegates from other campaigns through their state convention process.

It is considered easier to steal delegates in primary states than in caucus states because caucus states require a higher level of organization for the winning candidates and the voters are closer to the grassroots state convention process.

However, Iowa has historically proven to be an exception with Ron Paul over performing at the state convention in 2012 and winning the delegates that otherwise would have been assigned to Mitt Romney and Rick Santorum.

It is likely that one or more of the candidates choose to keep their Iowa organization together to try and elect SINOs to infiltrate opposing campaigns.

IOWA 2016

Numbers	Important Dates
30 Total Delegates **15 AL, 12 CD and 3 RNC**	**Presidential Preference Caucus: 2/1** **Precinct Caucuses: 2/1** **County Conventions: 3/12** **Congressional District Caucuses: 4/9** **State Convention: 5/21**
Selection Method	Allocation Details
AL – at State Convention **CD** – at Congressional District Caucuses	**AL & CD** – Proportional based on statewide vote with no threshold

- Strictly proportional
- If only one candidate's name is put in nomination at convention, then all delegates are bound to vote for that candidate.

the information provided in boxes in this section is from the RNC

The Early States: New Hampshire

We also classify New Hampshire as an early state for the same reasons as we classify Iowa as an early state. New Hampshire is far different than Iowa in how they elect their National Convention delegates. There is far less of a chance for SINOs in the New Hampshire delegation because the presidential campaigns submit their own list of delegates that are elected based on the results of the primary.

The delegates are allocated based on the proportion of the total with a 10% threshold, and any excess delegates are awarded to the winner of the primary. There will be a number of candidates who don't reach the 10% threshold, and therefore more excess delegates will be given to the winner of the New Hampshire primary.

It is important to note that the Super Delegates in New Hampshire are unbound and can support the candidate of their choice. Only states that are free agent states or early states have unbound Super Delegates.

NEW HAMPSHIRE 2016

Numbers	*Important Dates*
23 Total Delegates **14 AL, 6 CD and 3 RNC**	**Primary: 2/9 (tentative; set by Secretary of State)**
Selection Method	*Allocation Details*
AL & CD – Presidential candidates submit a slate of proposed delegates to Secretary of State	**AL & CD** – Proportional based on statewide vote with 10% threshold. Remaining delegates awarded to statewide winner.

The Early States: South Carolina

South Carolina has always been a very important state in the Republican presidential nomination process, but it is even more important this year because it is the only state before March 15th that does not use proportional delegate allocation.

Iowa and New Hampshire had the option of going winner-take-all because all the early states are exempted from calendar-based penalties.

The candidate who wins the South Carolina primary will win all 29 At-Large and Super Delegates (RNC Members) and therefore the winner of the South Carolina primary will without a doubt be the leader in the delegate totals at that stage of the calendar. The remaining 21 delegates will be given in increments of three to the plurality winner of each of the 7 congressional districts.

But South Carolina elects their delegates at a state convention. This means that SINOs are very possible to infiltrate the South Carolina delegation and candidates will have to work hard to get the right delegates elected.

SOUTH CAROLINA 2016

Numbers	*Important Dates*
50 Total Delegates **26 AL, 21 CD and 3 RNC**	**Primary: 2/20** **Precinct Conventions: March 2015** **County Conventions: April 2015 and March 2016 (if necessary)** **Congressional District Conventions: April 2016 (set by districts; can be no less than 5 days before state convention)** **State Convention: 5/7**
Selection Method	*Allocation Details*
AL – at State Convention	**AL** – Winner-take-all by statewide vote
CD – at Congressional District Conventions	**CD** – Winner-take-all by congressional district vote

The Early States: Nevada

Nevada is an early state and therefore deserves some respect in the nomination process. However, the media doesn't seem to take it seriously and therefore it doesn't have the impact of other early states in terms of generating momentum.

There have also been several recent controversies in Nevada and has a Republican Party organization that is considered one of the weaker state party organizations in the country. Nevada has been a contentious state since the Ron Paul organization attempted to take over the 2008 Nevada State Convention and essentially steal the delegates that McCain and Romney won by running Paul-aligned candidates for national delegate. This was the most public instance of SINOs in the last twenty years.

It is easy to point to Nevada as the reason why the RNC passed binding to the result of their presidential preference poll.

In 2016, delegates in Nevada will still be elected at a state convention and will be apportioned proportionally. Therefore no candidate is likely to get a majority of the delegates and there is a potential for SINOs again as there was in 2008 and 2012.

It should be noted that if a candidate drops or suspends then they have the option of releasing their delegates, or reallocating their delegates before the state convention.

NEVADA 2016

Numbers	*Important Dates*
30 Total Delegates 　　**15 AL, 12 CD and 3 RNC**	**Presidential Preference Caucus: 2/23** **County Convention: TBD** **State Convention: TBD**
Selection Method	*Allocation Details*
AL – at State Convention **CD** – by Congressional District Sessions at State Convention	**AL & CD** – Proportional based on statewide vote with no threshold

The Free Agents

The early states deserve their own classification, but the most important delegations at a contested Republican National Convention in 2016 will be the free agents. Colorado, North Dakota, Wyoming, American Samoa, Guam, Virgin Islands, and to some degree Louisiana are not necessarily restricted by RNC rules that pertain to a presidential preference poll.

Why are these small states so important in a contested convention? The answer is simple: They are free to make their own decisions.

1) They are free to elect convention committee members free from the influence of bound delegates. In many states the presidential campaigns will exert their influence over the delegates that they helped elect to vote for their choices for critical convention committees such as the Rules Committee.

2) They are free to vote to give ballot access to whichever candidates they want. They can sign nomination paperwork for whoever they want because they are not bound to the result of any preference poll.

3) They are free to vote however they want for president even when binding rules are still in effect. They don't have a presidential preference poll so there is no result to bind them. They can also change their votes from ballot to ballot regardless of when/whether the convention chooses to adjust its binding regulations.

4) They are free to exercise strategic voting to increase the power of SINOs, or minimize the power of SINOs. Momentum is a critical component of any multi-ballot race and these are the delegates that can help generate it with their ability to vote strategically to enhance, or limit, the power of SINOs.

Free agent delegations are not all created equally. The free agents are divided into two groups: unrestricted free agents and restricted free agents.

The Unrestricted Free Agents

They are completely unrestricted in who they support and how they vote at the national convention and are therefore the most powerful delegations on the floor of the convention.

The Free Agents: North Dakota

The most vocal of the three unrestricted free agent delegations is likely to be North Dakota. Curly Haugland is the longtime Republican National Committeeman and rabble rouser for the anti-establishment side of the Republican National Committee.

He has very forcefully pushed two big issues at RNC Meetings dating back to 2005. The first is that he is very vocal about the need for the RNC Chairman to be a member of the Republican National Committee. Technically the rules do not require it, and it became offensive to some members that George W. Bush kept endorsing candidates for RNC Chairman who were not in tune with the RNC Members. There is some value in having relationships with the membership, and that is why as Bush became a lame duck he turned to longtime member Mike Duncan rather than another White House operative to chair the RNC.

The second big issue that Haugland has been pushing in his decade on the RNC is to change the rules to make a presidential nomination controlled by national convention delegates and take the authority away from the media-controlled primary process. The chaos in Cleveland is in many ways the culmination of a decade's work for Mr. Haugland, and as a result, he will be a key RNC member and a leader of the most important delegation on the floor of the national convention.

North Dakota has 28 total free agent delegates whereas American Samoa and Guam each only have 9 free agent delegates. Therefore, North Dakota will arguably be the the most powerful delegation in Cleveland if they remain united.

NORTH DAKOTA 2016

Numbers	*Important Dates*
28 Total Delegates **22 AL, 3 CD and 3 RNC**	**District Caucuses: 1/1 – 3/1** **State Convention/Caucus: 4/1 – 4/3**
Selection Method	*Allocation Details*
AL & CD – at State Convention/Caucus	**AL & CD** – No preference vote. Delegates are unbound.

Here is how the delegates are elected:

Section 2. Delegates-Alternates to the Republican National Convention

In a Presidential election year, the Committee on Permanent Organization will present a slate of delegates and alternates to the State Republican Endorsing Convention from persons who applied to the committee from nomination. Any sitting Republican North Dakota State Governor, U.S. Senator, or U.S. Representative shall, without application to the committee, be deemed to have applied to the committee and shall be presented on the slate. Nominations may be made from the floor, and shall be added to the bottom of the ballot in the order nominated. Only those persons who applied to the committee, but were not nominated as a delegate will be eligible to be nominated from the floor. A nominee must finish in the top number needed for delegates to be elected. The same procedure will be followed for alternates to the Republican National Convention.

The Free Agents: Guam

Guam is an unrestricted free agent and the nine total delegates (including the three super delegate RNC members) are likely to follow the lead of Governor Calvo. Although Mr. Haugland of North Dakota will have more influence among RNC Members, there will likely be some national delegates from North Dakota who follow their own lead and don't necessarily vote as a bloc. Guam will be very likely to vote as a bloc led by Governor Calvo. Governor Calvo has endorsed Ted Cruz for President and the Cruz campaign was very wise to put the time and effort into gaining his endorsement. It could prove critically important.

GUAM 2016

Numbers	Important Dates
9 Total Delegates **6 AL and 3 RNC**	**Territorial Convention: 3/12**
Selection Method	*Allocation Details*
AL – at Territorial Convention	**AL** – No preference vote. Delegates are unbound.
CD – N/A	**CD** – N/A

The Free Agents: American Samoa

American Samoa is very similar to Guam in that the delegates are unbound and there is one elected official who has a very strong influence,

Amata Radewagen is the longest serving member of the RNC - first elected in 1986. She has served as a staffer for a number of well known Republican leaders including Congressman Phil Crane and Congressman J.C. Watts. She ran multiple times to represent American Samoa as at-large delegate to the United States House of Representatives, and won in 2014.

She is a very intelligent political leader and knows pretty much everyone at the highest levels of Republican politics. Her endorsement will be critical in a contested convention process and she will be one of the most important leaders at the convention. Keep an eye on Amata Radewagen.

AMERICAN SAMOA 2016

Numbers	Important Dates
9 Total Delegates **6 AL and 3 RNC**	**Territorial Caucus: 3/22**
Selection Method	Allocation Details
AL – at Territorial Caucus	**AL** – No preference vote. Delegates are unbound.
CD – N/A	
	CD – N/A

The Restricted Free Agents

The next group of delegations in terms of importance are the Restricted Free Agents. The Restricted Free Agents have more freedom than states that are bound by a presidential preference vote, but less freedom than North Dakota, American Samoa, and Guam. The most common restriction is that some (or possibly all depending on the results of their contests) of their delegates could be bound by a declaration that they make with their state party organization.

For example, the Virgin Islands delegation will be bound to the presidential candidate that they declare on their Declaration of Delegate Candidacy form, if any. But many candidates for delegate run unaffiliated to a campaign as they have in the past. For example, in 2008 all six delegates won as uncommitted even though John McCain received the most votes among the candidates.

The Restricted Free Agents: US Virgin Islands

Voters in the US Virgin Islands often think that their vote doesn't count because the Virgin Islands doesn't have Electoral Votes in the general election. Nothing could be further from the truth in 2016: The Virgin Islands will be one of the most important delegations on the floor of the national convention and registered Republicans can vote in the March 10th Caucus.

The Virgin Islands does not have a presidential preference poll and therefore has the ability to be a free agent delegation. But in order to be free, the delegates who are elected will need to run as "Unaffiliated" so that they are not bound by the results of the preference that they gave on their delegate form.

It would be a tremendous advantage to the Virgin Islands to elect a majority of its delegates as unaffiliated, and give the territory significant relevance at the national convention. If the delegates they elect are bound to a particular candidate, that would give the Virgin Islands delegation much less authority in committee assignments, ballot access, and of course the vote for President on the floor.

We will not know whether the Virgin Islands delegates are truly free until we know the results of the delegate elections and whether delegates made the mistake of declaring a candidate preference in advance.

VIRGIN ISLANDS 2016

Numbers	Important Dates
9 Total Delegates **6 AL and 3 RNC**	**Territorial Caucus: 3/10**
Selection Method	Allocation Details
AL – at Territorial Caucus CD – N/A	AL – No presidential preference vote. Delegates are bound to the presidential candidate they declare, if any, at the Territorial Caucus. CD – N/A

The Restricted Free Agents: Wyoming

Wyoming is very similar to the Virgin Islands in that delegates are not bound unless they declare a candidate preference at their state convention.

Wyoming would be well served to select delegates who do not declare a presidential preference at the state convention on April 16th.

WYOMING 2016

Numbers	Important Dates
29 Total Delegates 23 AL, 3 CD and 3 RNC	**Precinct Caucuses: 3/1** **County Conventions: 3/12** **State Convention: 4/16**

Selection Method	Allocation Details
AL – at State Convention **CD** – at County Conventions	**AL** – No presidential preference vote. Delegates are bound to the presidential candidate they declare, if any, at the State Convention. **CD** – No presidential preference vote. Delegates are bound to the presidential candidate they declare, if any, at the State Convention.

The Restricted Free Agents: Colorado

Colorado is very similar to the Virgin Islands and Wyoming and includes a box to check "unpledged" on their National Delegate Intent to Run form. Colorado would have far more influence in a contested national convention if they elected delegates who were not pledged to any presidential candidate.

COLORADO 2016

Numbers	Important Dates
37 Total Delegates 13 AL, 21 CD and 3 RNC	**Precinct Caucuses: 3/1** **County Assemblies: 3/1 – 3/26** **Congressional District Conventions: 3/29 – 4/8** **State Convention: 4/9**

Selection Method	Allocation Details
AL – at State Convention **CD** – at Congressional District Conventions	**AL** – No preference vote. Delegates are bound according to the preferred presidential candidate indicated on their intent to run form. **CD** – No preference vote. Delegates are bound according to the preferred presidential candidate indicated on their intent to run form.

NATIONAL DELEGATE INTENT TO RUN FORM

I, the undersigned, declare my candidacy to be a National Delegate from Colorado to the 2016 Republican National Convention, and file this notice of intent to run pursuant to Article XIII, § A (5)(a) of the Bylaws of the Colorado Republican State Central Committee and in accordance with applicable law and the Rules of the Republican Party.

I intend to stand for election as a candidate for National Delegate at the following convention(s):

☐ **Congressional District Convention – Congressional District #** _____

☐ **State Convention**

I understand that in order to elected as a National Delegate or National Alternate Delegate, I must be a qualified delegate or alternate delegate to the convention from which I seek to be elected. I also understand that I must be a resident of my precinct for thirty days and registered to vote no later than twenty-nine days prior to the precinct caucuses and affiliated with the Republican Party for at least two months prior to the precinct caucuses, or otherwise eligible to participate in the precinct caucuses, in order to be a candidate for National Delegate. I also must be continuously registered as a Republican elector in my congressional district or the state from February 1, 2016 until the convention, and I must have been a delegate, alternate delegate or qualified voting member of my county assembly in order to qualify as a candidate for National Delegate.

I further understand that in the event I fail to meet the eligibility requirements, or if I fail to be elected as a delegate or alternate delegate to the congressional district convention or to the state convention, I will be disqualified as a candidate for National Delegate.

Full Name_____

☐ PledgedtoSupportPresidentialCandidate:_____

☐ Unpledged   Date of Birth: _____

Residential Street Address: _____

City: _____, Colorado Zip: _____

Mailing Address (if different): _____ City: _____,
Colorado Zip: _____

Email Address: _____Home Phone: (_____)_____
Mobile Phone: (_____)_____

_____   _____
Signature of Candidate for National Delegate   Date

County: _____ Precinct #:_____

The Restricted Free Agents: Louisiana

Chairman Roger Villere of Louisiana is a longtime member of the RNC and one of the most astute members of the committee. He put forward a set of rules in Louisiana that has an interesting provision that allows a large number of their delegates to become free agents:

> The results of the March 24 Republican Presidential Preference Primary will determine the allocation of "at-large" delegates. If a presidential candidate receives at least 20% of the votes in the statewide Presidential Preference Primary, that candidate will be allocated at large delegates to the national convention in proportion to the percentage of votes received, rounded to the nearest delegate. All other at large delegates will be designated as uncommitted. If no candidate receives more than 20% of the votes in the Presidential Preference Primary, all at large delegates will be designated as uncommitted.

The delegates are allocated to presidential candidates in strict proportion to the percentage of the vote that each respective candidate receives. Each candidate must receive at least 20% of the vote in order to receive delegates. All other delegates go to the Republican National Convention as uncommitted, and therefore are free agents at the convention.

It is also possible, although not probable, that no candidate receives 20% and therefore all at-large delegates could be uncommitted free agents. Regardless there will certainly be some free agents in the Louisiana delegation representing the candidates who received less than 20%. This was very smart of Louisiana and Chairman Villere.

LOUISIANA 2016

Numbers	Important Dates
46 Total Delegates **25 AL, 18 CD and 3 RNC**	**Primary: 3/5** **Congressional District Caucus: 3/1** **State Convention: 3/12**
Selection Method	*Allocation Details*
AL – at State Convention	**AL** – Proportional based on statewide vote with a 20% threshold
CD – Congressional District Caucuses	**CD** – Proportional based on congressional district vote with no threshold

State Convention States

The states that elect their delegates through a party process such as state conventions, rather than directly on the ballot, are the states with the next most powerful delegations.

That is because the election is likely to go multiple ballots and the delegates elected by state convention will be free to switch to the candidate of their choice and no longer be bound, and are likely to make decisions with their own hearts and minds rather than taking orders from a presidential campaign.

They will be much more independent minded that delegates from states where the campaigns selected the delegates in advance.

State Convention State: Michigan

The Michigan State Convention will take place on April 9, 2016 and will elect Congressional District Delegates on Friday, April 8th and At-Large Delegates on Saturday April 9th.

We use Michigan as the first example because there is a long history of "delegate stealing" in Michigan as outlined in a previous section of this book.

It is very likely that people who support other candidates will run for delegate spots regardless of which candidate is allocated the delegate spots in the Michigan primary. For example, if Trump wins Michigan, it is certain that people who did not support Donald Trump will run for delegate to attempt to steal those delegate spots and create SINOs.

The Trump campaign would need an aggressive effort in all fourteen congressional districts to make sure their delegates were elected in each district that he won in the March 8th primary. This is very difficult to do because all of the districts caucus simultaneously.

MICHIGAN 2016

Numbers

59 Total Delegates
    14 AL, 42 CD and 3 RNC

Important Dates

Primary: 3/8
County Conventions: 3/22
Congressional District Caucuses: 4/8
State Convention: 4/9

Selection Method

AL – at State Convention

CD – at Congressional District Caucuses

Allocation Details

AL & CD – Proportional based on statewide vote with a 15% threshold. If no candidate reaches 15%, threshold drops to the percentage of votes received by the highest candidate minus 5%. If a candidate receives >50% of the statewide vote, winner-take-all.

State Convention State: Alaska

Alaska has a presidential preference caucus on March 1 that is the first step in their state convention process. This will result in a different type of delegate being elected than in a state whose preference vote is in a primary election. Electing delegates through a multi-step caucus process tends to limit the number of SINOs, but that isn't always the case such as in Iowa in 2012. The delegates in Alaska should be a fairly good representation of the preference poll results, however, it is still a state convention state where the delegates will have their own hearts and minds.

ALASKA 2016

Numbers

28 Total Delegates
    22 AL, 3 CD and 3 RNC

Important Dates

Presidential Preference Caucus: 3/1
State House Legislative Dist. Conventions: 3/1 – 3/29
State Convention: 4/28 – 4/30

Selection Method

AL & CD – at State Convention

Allocation Details

AL & CD – Proportional based on statewide vote with a 13% threshold

State Convention State: Arizona

Arizona is a very important state because it is relatively early in the process, taking place on March 22, and is winner-take-all.

As discussed previously, states that elect their delegates at a state convention following a primary are likely to have potential for disloyal delegates (SINOs) because the primary and convention processes aren't directly relational other than the classification of the delegates. This differs from state convention caucus states where a presidential preference poll at the caucus is the first step in the process.

The SINO problem has potential to be worse in Arizona than in any other state. Arizona has a long history of disagreement between the grassroots base of the party that elects its state party leaders and the candidates who are elected on the primary ballot. This has played out most publicly when Senator John McCain was opposed in his 2010 reelection campaign by much of the grassroots in Arizona. McCain later put together an organization to take the grassroots of the party back over by electing friendly people to positions of authority in the local party. It remains to be seen how that tension will continue to play out as the Arizona primary selects its winner and the state convention elects the corresponding delegates. It is possible - arguably very likely - that there is a very strong difference of opinion between the delegates who are elected at the state convention and the campaign of the winner of the primary.

Making matters worse, Arizona is winner-take-all which means there won't be delegates slots for supporters of campaigns who lose the primary.

For these reasons, Arizona is likely to be the land of many SINOs and is a state to watch on the convention floor regardless of who wins the important primary on March 22nd.

ARIZONA 2016

Numbers

58 Total Delegates
   28 AL, 27 CD and 3 RNC

Important Dates

Primary: 3/22
Congressional District Caucus: 3/26 – 4/9
State Convention: 4/30

Selection Method

AL – at State Convention

CD – by Congressional District Caucuses at
   State Convention

Allocation Details

AL & CD – Winner-take-all by statewide vote

Additional note: Arizona uses mail-in ballots that are distributed roughly a month before the election. Therefore, the majority of the voting in the Arizona primary will take place in mid-February around the time of the South Carolina primary. This means that the results of the Arizona primary are unlikely to be greatly influenced by the momentum of the earlier March states.

State Convention State: Arkansas

Arkansas will hold Congressional District Conventions on April 30 and will elect At-Large Delegates at the State Committee Meeting on May 14. There is somewhat less chance of SINOs in Arkansas than in Arizona because the At-Large Delegates are elected at a state committee meeting that has fewer people than a state convention. State Committee Meetings tend to be more establishment-oriented than state convention atmospheres.

ARKANSAS 2016

Numbers

40 Total Delegates
    25 AL, 12 CD and 3 RNC

Important Dates
Primary: 3/1
County Conventions: 3/7 – 3/25
Congressional District Conventions: 4/30
State Committee Meeting: 5/14

Selection Method

AL – at State Committee Meeting

CD – at Congressional District Conventions

Allocation Details

AL – Proportional based on statewide vote with a 15% threshold. Each candidate that reaches the 15% threshold receives one delegate. After that, if a candidate receives > 50% of the statewide vote, then allocated remaining AL delegates. If no majority winner, then remaining AL delegates allocated proportionally among candidates who reached the 15% threshold.

CD – Proportional based on congressional district vote with no threshold. If candidate receives >50% of congressional district vote, candidate receives all three CD delegates. Otherwise, highest vote-getter receives two delegates and second highest receives one.

State Convention State: Delaware

Delaware is a state that has seen a dramatic shift in the grassroots base of the Republican Party. Delaware was long represented by moderates such as Mike Castle. That changed in 2010 when Tea Party darling Christine O'Donnell upset the establishment and won the primary for U.S. Senate.

The Chairman of the RNC's Conservative Steering Committee is Delaware National Committeewoman Ellen Barrosse; goes to show that there is conservative leadership in Delaware. She replaced longtime committeewoman Priscilla Rakestraw who was the most senior member of the RNC.

There is a relatively good chance that the candidate voters select in the winner-take-all Delaware primary is not supported by the grassroots base of the party making it possible for SINOs to emerge in Delaware.

DELAWARE 2016

Numbers	Important Dates
16 Total Delegates **10 AL, 3 CD and 3 RNC**	**Primary: 4/26** **Convention District Mtgs: TBA** **State Convention: 4/29 – 4/30**
Selection Method	*Allocation Details*
AL & CD – at State Convention	**AL & CD** – Winner-take-all by statewide vote

District of Columbia

Washington, D.C. has historically held a presidential primary but this cycle is allocating their delegates based on the results of a March 12th State Convention. Because the preference poll takes place as part of the convention process, it is unlikely that SINOs will emerge in D.C. However, Washington, D.C. is prime territory for a moderate to over-perform in a state convention process.

It is usually assumed that a State Convention process would lead to a more conservative delegation because the grassroots base of the party tends to be more conservative than primary voters. However, this is not necessarily the case in our nation's capital.

Washington, D.C. is very unique. There is a very high state-level tax and therefore most Republicans with flexibility of where to spend the majority of their time and declare their residency choose not to to declare it in Washington, D.C.

Additionally, the Republicans who do live there include a sizable number of GOP staffers. They tend to be much more moderate or libertarian-leaning on social issues- especially gay marriage- than your average GOP activist across the country who attends a state convention.

Washington, D.C. might be the one state convention in the country where the more moderate candidates outperform the more conservative candidates.

DISTRICT OF COLUMBIA 2016

Numbers	Important Dates
19 Total Delegates **16 AL and 3 RNC**	**Presidential Preference Convention: 3/12**
Selection Method	*Allocation Details*
AL – at Districtwide Convention **CD** – N/A	**AL** – Proportional based on district-wide vote with a 15% threshold. If no candidate reaches 15%, the threshold becomes 10%. If no candidate reaches 10%, the threshold becomes 8%. If candidate receives >50% of the district-wide vote, winner-take-all. **CD** – N/A

Florida

Florida will be one of the more interesting delegations because it is ground zero of the presidential race. It is the first and biggest state to go winner-take-all on March 15. Three competitive presidential candidates- Jeb Bush, Marco Rubio, and Donald Trump - all have strong ties to the state. There is a highly competitive U.S. Senate primary that is shaping up to be the defining establishment vs. anti-establishment primary in the country.

It is highly likely that several of the delegates who are elected at District Caucuses and at the State Executive Committee Meeting will be SINOs regardless of who wins the presidential primary.

FLORIDA 2016

Numbers	Important Dates
99 Total Delegates **15 AL, 81 CD and 3 RNC**	**Primary: 3/15** **Congressional District Caucuses: 3/22 – 6/3** **State Exec. Meeting: 3/22 – 6/3**
Selection Method	*Allocation Details*
AL – at State Executive Committee Meeting **CD** – at Congressional District Caucuses	**AL & CD** – Winner-take-all by statewide vote

178

Georgia

There doesn't tend to be as great a disparity on the ideological spectrum between the average primary voter and the average grassroots activist in most southern primaries. The most conservative candidates will tend to do well in the primary elections, and the most conservative candidates will tend to do well in the state conventions. Therefore, there isn't as much of a likelihood for SINOs in states like Georgia as there is in a state like Arizona.

GEORGIA 2016

Numbers

76 Total Delegates
    31 AL, 42 CD and 3 RNC

Important Dates

Primary: 3/1
Precinct Meetings: 2/11-2/20 & 3/10-3/19
County Conventions: 3/19
Congressional District Conventions: 4/16
State Convention: 6/3 – 6/4

Selection Method

AL – at State Convention

CD – at Congressional District Conventions

Allocation Details

AL – Proportional based on statewide vote with a 20% threshold. If no candidate reaches 20%, threshold becomes 15%. If no candidate reaches 15%, threshold becomes 10%. If a candidate receives >50% of statewide vote, candidate receives all AL delegates.

CD – Proportional based on congressional district vote with no threshold. If candidate receives >50% of the congressional district vote, candidate receives all three CD delegates. Otherwise, the highest vote-getter awarded two delegates and the second highest awarded one.

Idaho

Idaho had a highly controversial convention process in 2012 that supporters of Ron Paul attempted to overrun. As a result, Idaho made several rules changes to tighten their state convention process, and is holding a primary election on March 1. In a state like Idaho, conservative and Libertarian-leaning candidates will do well in both primaries and state conventions, and so there is likely to be some symmetry between the primary winner and the delegates who are elected at the state convention. However, there is still potential for liberty-leaning activists to win the state convention delegate slots regardless of the primary results.

IDAHO 2016

<u>Numbers</u>

32 Total Delegates
    23 AL, 6 CD and 3 RNC

<u>Important Dates</u>

Primary: 3/8
Precinct Conventions: 5/17
County Conventions: 5/20 – 5/28
State Convention: 6/2 – 6/4

<u>Selection Method</u>

AL & CD – at State Convention. Candidates submit slate of proposed delegates to state convention nominating committee; State Convention approves.

<u>Allocation Details</u>

AL & CD – Proportional based on statewide vote with 20% threshold. If no candidate reaches 20%, becomes directly proportional. If a candidate receives > 50% of the statewide vote, winner-take-all.

Indiana

Indiana is different than most state convention states in that it makes its party decisions at a state committee meeting rather than at a state convention. This generally leads to more establishment-oriented decision-making. Still, Indiana is a conservative state and there is potential for SINOs given that the supporters of candidates who lose the Indiana primary will still be looking for delegate slots in what is supposed to be a winner-take-all state.

INDIANA 2016

<u>Numbers</u>

57 Total Delegates
    27 AL, 27 CD and 3 RNC

<u>Important Dates</u>

Primary: 5/3
Congressional District Committee Mtgs: 4/9
State Committee Meeting: 4/13

<u>Selection Method</u>

AL – at State Committee Meeting

CD – by Congressional District Committees

<u>Allocation Details</u>

AL – Winner-take-all based on statewide vote

CD – Winner-take-all based on congressional district vote

180

Kansas

Kansas is a socially conservative state that will favor a conservative candidate. The preference poll is part of their state convention process and therefore it is likely that the delegates who are elected will be true to the candidates who win delegates in the Kansas process. That said, there is history of civil war between the conservative and moderate factions within the state and that could easily flare up again in 2016.

KANSAS 2016

Numbers	Important Dates
40 Total Delegates 25 AL, 12 CD and 3 RNC	**Presidential Preference Caucus: 3/5** **Congressional District Convention: 3/26 – 4/23** **State Convention: 4/24 – 5/21**
Selection Method	*Allocation Details*
AL – by State Committee at State Convention CD – by District Committee at Congressional District Convention	AL – Proportional based on statewide vote with a 10% threshold. If no candidate reaches 10%, becomes directly proportional. CD – Proportional based on congressional district vote with a 10% threshold. RNC – 3 RNC members bound to statewide winner

Kentucky

Kentucky usually has a primary but changed its process this cycle in order to allow Senator Rand Paul to run for both president and U.S. Senate simultaneously.

It has been ground zero in several establishment vs. anti-establishment battles over the last few cycles with Senator Mitch McConnell as a lighting rod for the establishment. A more conservative candidate is likely to win the caucus, and the delegates elected are likely to be in sync with the result because the preference poll is part of the state convention process. But Senator McConnell remains a wild card.

KENTUCKY 2016

Numbers

46 Total Delegates
    25 AL, 18 CD and 3 RNC

Important Dates

Presidential Preference Caucus: 3/5
County Meetings: 3/6 - 3/31
Congressional District Conventions: 4/1 - 5/17
State Convention: Before 5/18

Selection Method

AL – at State Convention

CD – at Congressional District Conventions

Allocation Details

AL & CD – Proportional based on statewide vote with a 5% threshold

Maine

Maine has been one of the more controversial state convention states during the past two presidential campaigns. The delegates to the Maine State Conventions tend to be more establishment-oriented, but there has been a very strong contingent of Ron Paul supporters who bring liberty-leaning organization to the state convention process. However, because the preference poll is part of the state convention process, the opportunities for SINOs is limited. But there always seems to be plenty of noise coming out of Maine.

MAINE 2016

Numbers

23 Total Delegates
    14 AL, 6 CD and 3 RNC

Important Dates

Presidential Preference Caucus: 3/5
Congressional District Caucuses: 4/21 – 4/23
State Convention: 4/21 – 4/23

Selection Method

AL – at State Convention

CD – at Congressional District Caucuses at State Convention

Allocation Details

AL & CD – Proportional based on statewide vote with a 10% threshold. If no candidate reaches 10%, the threshold becomes 5%. If a candidate receives >50% of the statewide vote, winner-take-all.

Maryland

Maryland is a winner-take-all state and therefore it is likely that there are supporters of candidates who lose the primary who want to attend the National Convention and therefore become SINOs. It is likely that a more moderate candidate wins the Maryland primary and that could create an opportunity for conservatives to steal delegates at the state convention.

MARYLAND 2016

Numbers	*Important Dates*
38 Total Delegates	**Primary: 4/26**
11 AL, 24 CD and 3 RNC	**State Convention: 5/14**
Selection Method	*Allocation Details*
AL – at State Convention by State Central Committee	**AL** –Winner-take-all based on statewide vote
CD – Elected on the primary ballot	**CD** –Winner-take-all based on congressional district vote

Massachusetts

Massachusetts was a very controversial battleground in 2012 and the same thing could happen again in 2016. Ron Kaufman is the very well respected National Committeeman who is practically the definition of the national GOP establishment as former George H.W. Bush's White House Political Director and longtime RNC insider. Supporters of Ron Paul fought him aggressively in 2012 and it will be interesting to watch whether something similar happens in 2016. Massachusetts has an important March 1st Primary that will be highly targeted by more moderate candidates.

MASSACHUSETTS 2016

Numbers	*Important Dates*
42 Total Delegates	**Primary: 3/1**
12 AL, 27 CD and 3 RNC	**Congressional District Caucus: 4/23**
	State Committee Mtg.: Between 5/1 and 6/3
Selection Method	*Allocation Details*
AL – at State Committee Meeting	**AL & CD** – Proportional based on statewide vote with a 5% threshold
CD – at Congressional District Caucuses	

Minnesota

Minnesota is a critical March 1st state that gives a conservative a good opportunity for a victory in the Midwest. The Minnesota preference poll is part of the state convention process and therefore it is likely that the delegates who are elected are relatively true to the candidates who win delegates. However, there is plenty of potential for acrimony at the state convention. There were reports of physicality in 2008, and 2016 could be no different. Keep an eye on Minnesota.

MINNESOTA 2016

Numbers	Important Dates
38 Total Delegates **11 AL, 24 CD and 3 RNC**	**Presidential Preference Caucus: 3/1** **County Caucuses: 3/12 – 4/11** **Congressional District Conventions: 4/22 – 5/7** **State Convention: 5/20**
Selection Method	*Allocation Details*
AL – at State Convention	**AL** – Proportional based on statewide vote with a 10% threshold. If a candidate receives >85% of the statewide vote, candidate receives all AL and CD delegates.
CD – at Congressional District Conventions	**CD** – Proportional based on congressional district vote with a 10% threshold

Mississippi

Mississippi is similar to other southern states in that a conservative is likely to win the state and the delegates that come out of the convention process are likely to be conservative as well. However, it is unique in that the family of former RNC Chairman Haley Barbour is heavily engaged in state politics and the recent U.S. Senate primary created bad blood between the grassroots and establishment in the state. Outsiders tend to do well in these battles around the country but don't bet against anyone with the last name of Barbour in Mississippi.

Mississippi probably has more capacity for SINOs than most southern states that have state conventions, but there is still likely to be symmetry in ideology between the winner of the primary and the delegates who are elected at the state convention. The Barbour/outsider divide will be something to watch closely.

MISSISSIPPI 2016

<u>Numbers</u>

40 Total Delegates
    25 AL, 12 CD and 3 RNC

<u>Important Dates</u>

Primary: 3/8
Precinct Caucuses: 4/23
Congressional District Caucuses: 5/13 – 5/14
State Convention: 5/13 – 5/14

<u>Selection Method</u>

AL – at State Convention

CD – by Congressional District Caucuses at
    State Convention

<u>Allocation Details</u>

AL – Proportional based on statewide vote with
    a 15% threshold. If no candidate reaches
    15%, threshold becomes 10%.

CD – Proportional based on congressional
    district vote. Highest vote-getter receives
    two delegates and second highest receives
    one. If a candidate receives >50% of the
    congressional district vote, candidate
    receives all three CD delegates.

Missouri

Missouri is March 15th but chose not to allocate their delegates winner- take-all unless a candidate gets over 50% of the vote in the primary election.

The delegates will be elected at a state convention in May providing considerable opportunity for delegates to be elected at the convention who are not necessarily supportive of the candidate who won the primary. There is a history of SINO's in Missouri and this year is likely to have a similar result.

MISSOURI 2016

Numbers	*Important Dates*
52 Total Delegates	**Primary: 3/15**
25 AL, 24 CD and 3 RNC	**Local/County Caucuses: 4/9**
	District Conventions: 4/30
	State Convention: 5/21

Selection Method	*Allocation Details*
AL – at State Convention	AL & CD – Proportional based on congressional district vote with the plurality winner of each CD receiving 5 delegates (3 CD & 2 AL) and the remaining 9 AL delegates given to the statewide plurality winner. If a candidate receives >50% of the statewide vote, winner-take-all.
CD – at Congressional District Conventions	

Montana

Montana has a winner-take-all primary on June 7 that will take place after the selection of National Convention delegates on May 14. Therefore, it is almost guaranteed that some of the delegates will not be supportive of the primary victor. Therefore several of the Montana delegates will likely be SINOs.

MONTANA 2016

Numbers	*Important Dates*
27 Total Delegates	**Primary: 6/7**
21 AL, 3 CD and 3 RNC	**State Delegate Convention: 5/14**

Selection Method	*Allocation Details*
AL – at State Delegate Convention	AL & CD – Winner-take-all based on statewide vote
CD – at State Delegate Convention	

Nebraska

Nebraska has a winner-take-all primary in May with the election of National Convention delegates four days later at the state convention. It is possible that some of the delegates elected at the state convention will not necessarily be strong supporters of the winner of the primary. This tends to be the case in winner-take-all states because there are some activists who will expect to go to the convention regardless of who wins the primary.

NEBRASKA 2016

Numbers	_Important Dates_
36 Total Delegates **24 AL, 9 CD and 3 RNC**	**Primary: 5/10** **County Conventions: 4/1 – 4/10** **State Convention: 5/14**
Selection Method	_Allocation Details_

AL – at State Convention
 	
CD – at Congressional District Caucuses at State
     Convention
	AL & CD – Winner-take-all based on statewide
	     vote

New Mexico

New Mexico is another state that, uniquely, elects their delegates prior to the primary election. It is therefore certain that several of the delegates won't necessarily be supporters of the candidate who wins the primary.

NEW MEXICO 2016

Numbers	_Important Dates_
24 Total Delegates **12 AL, 9 CD and 3 RNC**	**Primary: 6/7** **County Conventions: 1/16 – 1/30; 4/16 – 4/30** **State Convention: 5/21**
Selection Method	_Allocation Details_
AL & CD – at State Convention	**AL & CD** – Proportional based on statewide vote with a 15% threshold

New York

New York will likely be able to keep tighter control of their delegation because it is a proportional state with a large delegation and therefore will have slots for key supporters of the candidates who win delegates in the primary election. Additionally, delegates are elected at a state committee meeting rather than at a state convention, and that tends to be easier for party leaders to control.

NEW YORK 2016

Numbers	_Important Dates_
95 Total Delegates **11 AL, 81 CD and 3 RNC**	**Primary: 4/19** **State Committee Mtg: 5/18**
Selection Method	_Allocation Details_
AL – by State Committee	**AL** – Proportional based on statewide vote with a 20% threshold. If candidate receives > 50% of the statewide vote, candidate receives all AL delegates.
CD – by State Committee representing each Congressional District	**CD** – Proportional based on congressional district vote with 20% threshold. Highest vote-getter receives two delegates and second highest receives one. If a candidate receives >50% of the congressional district vote, candidate receives all three CD delegates.

North Carolina

North Carolina is a proportional state and therefore there should be room for key supporters of the major candidates to be elected as delegates to keep the delegation relatively in sync with the results of the primary.

However, depending on the ideology of the winner of the North Carolina primary there could be potential for SINOs.

North Carolina 2016

Numbers	Important Dates
72 Total Delegates **30 AL, 39 CD and 3 RNC**	**Primary: 3/15** **Precinct Conventions: February 2016** **County Conventions: March 2016** **Congressional District Conventions: April 2016** **State Convention: 5/5 – 5/8**

Selection Method	Allocation Details
AL – at State Convention **CD** – at Congressional District Conventions	**AL & CD** – Proportional based on statewide vote with no threshold

Northern Marianas Islands

Northern Marianas have a caucus on March 15th that also elected delegates to the on the same day. The delegates are bound to the result of the preference poll. It is likely that the winner of the preference poll will have the loyalty of the delegates who are elected that day. Ben Carson advisor Jason Osborne is a critical player in this process as the Executive Director of the NMI GOP.

Northern Mariana Islands 2016

Numbers	Important Dates
9 Total Delegates **6 AL and 3 RNC**	**Presidential Preference Caucus: 3/15**

Selection Method	Allocation Details
AL – at Territorial Caucus **CD** – N/A	**AL** – Winner-take-all **CD** – N/A

Oklahoma

Oklahoma is a relatively conservative state whose primary voters are relatively in sync with the grassroots base of the party. It is proportional so there should be spots for supporters of each candidate who wins delegates.

OKLAHOMA 2016

Numbers

43 Total Delegates
  25 AL, 15 CD and 3 RNC

Important Dates

Primary: 3/1
Precinct Meeting: 2/9
County Conventions: Before 3/12
Congressional District Conventions: Before 4/17
State Convention: 5/13 – 5/14

Selection Method

AL – at State Convention

CD – at Congressional District Conventions

Allocation Details

AL – Proportional based on statewide vote with a 15% threshold. If a candidate receives > 50% of statewide vote, candidate receives all AL delegates.

CD – Proportional based on congressional district vote with 15% threshold. If only one candidate >15%, candidate receives all three CD delegates. If two candidates >15%, the highest vote-getter receives two delegates and the second highest receives one. If three or more candidates >15%, top three candidates receive one delegate each. If a candidate receives > 50% of the congressional district vote, candidate receives all three CD delegates.

Oregon

Oregon hasn't been significantly impacted by the grassroots outsider takeovers that have happened in other states across the country. It is likely that the results of the primary are relatively in tune with the delegates who are elected at the state convention.

OREGON 2016

Numbers	*Important Dates*
28 Total Delegates	**Primary: 5/17**
10 AL, 15 CD and 3 RNC	**State Convention: 6/4**
Selection Method	*Allocation Details*
AL – at State Convention	AL & CD – Proportional by allocating one delegate for every 4% of the statewide vote
CD – by Congressional District Conventions at State Convention	

South Dakota

South Dakota is a winner-take-all state that is selecting its delegates a full three months before its June primary. Therefore it is almost certain that delegates elected at the delegate selection meeting will not necessarily all support the winner of the primary election.

SOUTH DAKOTA 2016

Numbers	*Important Dates*
29 Total Delegates	**Primary: 6/7**
23 AL, 3 CD and 3 RNC	**Regional Caucuses: 3/1 – 3/10**
	Delegate Selection Meeting: 3/19
Selection Method	*Allocation Details*
AL & CD – At State National Convention Delegate Selection Meeting	AL & CD – Winner-take-all based on statewide vote

Texas

Texas has a very interesting allocation system. If the winning candidate receives over 50% of the vote then they receive all the at-large delegates, and if the winning candidate in a congressional district gets over 50%, then that candidate wins all 3 district delegates.

There isn't likely to be much difference between the results of the primary and the types of delegates who are elected at the state convention because Texas is a very conservative state with a state convention and primary.

TEXAS 2016

Numbers

155 Total Delegates
    44 AL, 108 CD and 3 RNC

Important Dates

Primary: 3/1
Precinct Conventions: TBD
District Conventions: 3/19
State Convention: 5/12 – 5/14

Selection Method

AL – at State Convention

CD – by Congressional District Caucuses at State Convention

Allocation Details

AL – Proportional based on statewide vote with a 20% threshold. If only one candidate reaches the 20% threshold, then the second highest vote-getter is also proportionally allocated delegates. If no candidate reaches 20%, becomes directly proportional. If a candidate receives > 50% of statewide vote, candidate receives all AL delegates.

CD – Proportional based on congressional district vote with a 20% threshold. If only one candidate reaches 20%, highest vote-getter receives two delegates and second highest receives one. If two candidates reach 20%, highest vote-getter receives two delegates and second highest receives one. If no candidates reaches 20%, top three candidates receive one delegate each. If candidate receives >50% of congressional district vote, candidate receives all three CD delegates.

Utah

The Utah preference poll is part of the state convention process and therefore the delegates elected are likely to be congruent to the results of the presidential preference poll.

UTAH 2016

Numbers	Important Dates
40 Total Delegates **25 AL, 12 CD and 3 RNC**	**Presidential Preference Caucus: 3/22** **Precinct Caucuses: 3/22** **Congressional District Caucuses: 4/23** **State Convention: 4/23**
Selection Method	Allocation Details
AL – at State Convention CD – at Congressional District Caucuses at State Convention	AL & CD – Proportional based on statewide vote with 15% threshold. If less than three candidates reach the threshold, the threshold becomes zero and delegates are allocated directly proportional. If a candidate receives > 50% of the statewide vote, winner-take-all.

Vermont

Vermont is a very moderate state with a state convention. Usually this would be a formula for SINOs but Vermont hasn't had much in the way of a conservative grassroots uprising in recent history.

VERMONT 2016

Numbers	Important Dates
16 Total Delegates **10 AL, 3 CD and 3 RNC**	**Primary: 3/1** **Precinct Caucuses: TBD** **State Convention: 5/21**
Selection Method	Allocation Details
AL & CD – at State Convention	AL & CD – Proportional based on statewide vote with a 20% threshold. If no candidate reaches 20%, threshold becomes 15%. If no candidate reaches 15%, threshold becomes 10%. If a candidate receives > 50% of the statewide vote, winner-take-all.

Virginia

Virginia is a state ripe for SINOs because the convention is relatively unruly and will not necessarily conform to the results of the March 1st primary. There are several critical national players in Virginia including Republican National Committeeman Morton Blackwell, as well as consultants Mike Rothfeld and Chris LaCivita. Keep an eye on Virginia.

VIRGINIA 2016

Numbers	Important Dates
49 Total Delegates **13 AL, 33 CD and 3 RNC**	**Primary: 3/1** **City & County Meetings: 2/6 – 4/11** **Congressional District Conventions: Before May 23** **State Convention: 4/30**
Selection Method	Allocation Details
AL – at State Convention **CD** – at Congressional District Conventions	**AL & CD** – Proportional based on statewide vote with no threshold

Washington

Washington has always been a hotly contested state in the state convention phase of the presidential campaign and this year is likely to be no different. The 2012 nomination campaign shifted to a battle of state conventions around the time of the Washington convention and Ron Paul supporters and Rick Santorum supporters attempted to team up to defeat Mitt Romney.

There will likely be several SINOs in Washington State because the election of delegates actually happens prior to the presidential primary.

WASHINGTON 2016

Numbers

44 Total Delegates
    11 AL, 30 CD and 3 RNC

Selection Method

AL – at State Convention

CD – by Congressional District Caucuses at
    State Convention

Important Dates

Primary: 5/24
Precinct Conventions: 2/20
County Conventions: 3/12 – 4/16
Congressional District Caucuses: 5/19 – 5/21
State Convention: 5/19 – 5/21

Allocation Details

AL – Proportional based on statewide vote with
    a 20% threshold

CD – Proportional based on congressional
    district vote with 20% threshold. If
    candidate receives >50%, candidate
    receives all three CD delegates. If no
    candidate over 20%, top three vote-getters
    each receive a delegate. If only one
    candidate over 20%, candidate receives
    three delegates. If two candidates over
    20%, highest vote-getter receives two
    delegates and second highest receives
    one. If three candidates over 20%, each
    candidate receives one delegate. If four
    candidates over 20%, top three vote-
    getters receive one delegate each.

Wisconsin

Wisconsin is a winner-take-all state and therefore there will be several supporters of candidates who lose the primary who still want to attend the convention and will run at the district caucuses and state committee meeting.

WISCONSIN 2016

Numbers

42 Total Delegates
    15 AL, 24 CD and 3 RNC

Selection Method

AL – at State Executive Committee Meeting

CD – at Congressional District Caucuses

Important Dates

Primary: 4/5
County Caucuses: TBD
Congressional District Caucuses: 4/6 – 4/17
State Executive Committee Meeting: 5/14

Selection Details

AL – Winner-take-all based on statewide vote

CD – Winner-take-all based on congressional
    district vote

Convention/Ballot Hybrids

There are some states that are hybrids between state convention-selected delegates and delegates who are elected on the primary ballot.

Illinois

The statewide delegates are winner-take-all based on the statewide results of the primary election. Therefore there are likely to be several SINOs elected at the state convention. The District Delegates however are directly elected on the ballot and therefore are likely to be in sync with the candidate who won delegates in their district.

ILLINOIS 2016

Numbers	*Important Dates*
69 Total Delegates	**Primary: 3/15**
12 AL, 54 CD and 3 RNC	**State Convention: 5/20 – 5/22**
Selection Method	*Allocation Details*
AL – at State Convention	**AL** – Winner-take-all based on statewide vote
CD – Elected on the primary ballot	**CD** – Elected on the primary ballot and bound to the candidate for whom they declare

Pennsylvania

Pennsylvania is similar to Illinois in that the statewide delegates are winner-take-all based on the results of the statewide primary, and the district delegates are elected on the ballot.

However, in Pennsylvania the At-Large Delegates are elected at a state committee meeting rather than a state convention. Therefore there is somewhat less chance of SINO's.

PENNSYLVANIA 2016

Numbers	_Important Dates_
71 Total Delegates 14 AL, 54 CD and 3 RNC	**Primary: 4/26** **State Committee Meeting: 5/21**
Selection Method	_Allocation Details_
AL – at State Committee Meeting	**AL** – Winner-take-all based on statewide vote
CD – Elected on the primary ballot	**CD** – Elected on the primary ballot as officially unbound

Tennessee

Tennessee is very unique in that the At-Large delegates are elected on the primary ballot but are selected by the state executive committee. A cynic would argue that this creates the possibility for the executive committee to pick delegates of questionable allegiance but historically the party has handled this process fairly.

TENNESSEE 2016

Numbers	_Important Dates_
58 Total Delegates 28 AL, 27 CD and 3 RNC	**Primary: 3/1** **State Exec. Committee Mtg.: 4/2**
Selection Method	_Allocation Details_
AL –14 AL delegates are elected on primary ballot; 14 AL delegates are selected by State Executive Committee. **CD** – Elected on the primary ballot	**AL** – Proportional based on statewide vote with a 20% threshold. If no candidate reaches 20%, becomes directly proportional. If a candidate receives > 66% of statewide vote, candidate receives all AL delegates. **CD** – Proportional based on congressional district vote with 20% threshold. If candidate receives > 66% of the congressional district vote, candidate receives all three CD delegates. If winner receives 20-66% of the vote, highest vote-getter receives two delegates and second highest receives one, unless the second place candidate has < 20% of the vote, then candidate receives all three. If no candidate reaches 20%, top three candidates each receive one delegate.

Balloted and Campaign Selected Delegates

States that elect their delegates on the primary ballot will tend to have delegates who are loyal to the campaign that earns them because the campaign was involved in recruiting those delegates. Included in this list are states in which the campaigns outright select the delegates.

The following states have delegates who are elected on the ballot:

Ohio
Alabama
New Jersey
Puerto Rico
Rhode Island
West Virginia

The following states have delegates that are filed by the campaigns:

California
Connecticut
Hawaii

There is significantly less risk for campaigns who won delegates within the nine delegations listed above because the campaigns were involved in the selection process.

This leads to a significantly different type of delegate than in a state such as Michigan that elects their delegates at a state convention.

There will be relatively few, if any, SINO's in these balloted delegations.

18. National Convention Ballots

The balloting process at the national convention is such that the roll of the states is called and every state announces their vote total. The totals that are announced must be congruent to the binding rules that are in effect, otherwise the announced result will be ignored. State delegations may pass and then make their announcement after the other states have made their respective announcements. If no candidate receives a majority, then the roll of the states occurs again, and keeps occurring until a candidate receives a majority.

The rules do not dictate at what point the binding of the states is lifted. For example, if binding is not lifted, the roll of states will not change much between balloting rounds because only the free agents can change their minds.

Eventually something will be done to lift the binding, either through the Rules committee process or by suspension of the rules on the floor. But if the candidate who has a plurality lead on the floor does not allow the rules to be changed, then total chaos will ensue.

Multiple Ballots
The vote will almost certainly go multiple ballots for the reasons outlined in the beginning of this book. This makes it critically important that campaigns are involved in the election of delegates at state conventions across the country, and properly filed supporters as delegates in states that required it.

Those campaigns who failed to run their own delegates in states such as Alabama will be at a severe disadvantage in a contested convention fight because even the delegates who are bound to vote for them on early ballots based on the new RNC rules won't be loyal to them on later ballots after the binding is eventually lifted.

The candidates who do the best job of getting their supporters elected at state conventions, even if those supporters are bound to other candidates, will have tremendous - and possibly determinative - advantage at the national convention.

The closest example of this type of multiple ballot scenario in an RNC contest would be the RNC Chairman races over the last 20 years. All of those contested elections went multiple ballots with the exception of Jim Nicholson's victory over Tom Slade in 1999.

Momentum

There is nothing more important than momentum from ballot to ballot in winning a multi-ballot convention race. This has been exemplified in races for RNC Chairman over the last 20 years. A candidate who goes from 20 votes to 25 votes is in far greater position than a candidate who goes from 30 votes to 26 votes. Momentum matters as much, or more, than the actual vote count. This is a similar concept to over-performing or under-performing expectations in an early state contest such as Iowa, New Hampshire, or South Carolina.

SINOs will have a dramatic impact on the momentum swings from ballot to ballot as more and more delegations are able to vote with their hearts and minds rather than being limited by the binding rules of the RNC and their respective state allocations rules.

19. Key Players

It is true that every delegate has one vote and that the delegates run the convention, but there are some key players who hold influence over segments of delegates. For example, party leaders have influence over the delegates who elected them leaders, social conservative leaders have influence with social conservatives, establishment leaders have influence with establishment delegates, and libertarian leaders have influence with libertarian-leaning delegates.

Party Leaders

Party Leaders are elected by the grassroots of their party in their respective states and therefore generally have some level of influence over the activists who are in the state delegations. However, this varies dramatically by state, and generally party leaders have less authority in a post-2008 world that is dominated by the outsider side of the spectrum.

RNC Members are party leaders by definition and are the most important players in the Republican National Convention process. They make up the Committee on Arrangements (COA) that sets up the convention, passes rules, makes recommendations on credentials challenges, and generally have support among the state delegations who elected them to positions of leadership. They also tend to have the ear of the RNC Chairman who they elected as their leader.

Social Conservative Leaders

The last great divide in the Republican Party was over the heart and soul of the party on social conservative issues such as abortion. Many of the troops in those battles integrated into positions of leadership within the party and others became conservative leaders outside the party structure.

Although the party has largely become a social conservative party and coopted many of the issues of the social conservative movement, there are still some leaders who have a great deal of respect and authority among the delegates.

Phyllis Schlafly is probably the most influential conservative non-member of the Republican National Committee. She and Colleen Paro led a group called RNC for Life that successfully fought to keep the pro-life plank in the Republican Party Platform for decades. There are also a number of Republican National Committeewomen across the country who are members of Eagle Forum and therefore have some loyalty to Phyllis Schlafly and her organization. When she speaks, conservative delegates listen. There is an upcoming race for RNC Chairman after this election and that will give her increased authority with the potential RNC Chairman candidates as well.

There are other social conservative leaders with influence such as Gary Bauer, James Dobson, Tony Perkins, and numerous others.

Establishment Leaders

The establishment is nowhere near as powerful as it was in past conventions and, by definition, the establishment could change with a new nominee or even a presumptive nominee.

But there are people who are viewed as establishment leaders such as Massachusetts Committeeman Ron Kaufman, Attorney Ben Ginsberg, Karl Rove, and many of the Governors and US Senators across the country who will have an impact over establishment-minded voters on the convention floor.

But these folks are not able to implement their will over the committee process or delegations like they could at past conventions. The dominance of the outsider spectrum among the grassroots base of the party and the delegations' respective loyalties to their preferred candidates will dramatically limit their authority.

Liberty Leaders

Ron Paul has been one of the most influential people at the previous two conventions and will continue to be important in the lead up to the 2016 national convention. There are also a few RNC members who are liberty-leaning and therefore will listen to Ron Paul on various items of consequence.

Media

All members of the media are not created equally when it comes to understanding a convoluted and difficult convention process. There are some journalists who have spent more time than others at RNC meetings and conventions over the years and have developed relationships with other key players.

Ralph Hallow – Ralph Hallow is a longtime reporter for the Washington Times who has spent social time with RNC Members at RNC Meetings across the country for decades.

Chuck Todd - Chuck Todd may work for liberal-leaning NBC, but he has a strong knowledge of the inner workings of Republican Party election contests going back to his days covering the 1997 election for RNC Chairman at PoliticsNow.com.

John Gizzi - John Gizzi is a longtime reporter for Human Events who now reports for Newsmax.com. He knows more about the local GOP politics in various states across the country than probably any reporter in America. He is a longtime fixture at CPAC and Republican National Committee meetings.

Reid Wilson – Reid Wilson is a former reporter for Hotline and the Washington Post who is now the lead reporter for Morning Consult. He has spent a great deal of time covering past RNC Chairman elections and knows the relationships among the members very well.

20. Prisoners' Dilemma

"Just because I am paranoid doesn't mean there aren't black helicopters flying overhead."

The intellectual sport of game theory has a "prisoners' dilemma" that describes a situation where there are two players who are each trying to maximize their own benefit. If both remain loyal to each other (keep quiet and neither confesses to a crime) then they will both enjoy the optimal outcome (get out of jail). The dilemma happens when the players lose trust for one another and try to maximize their position (making a deal to confess), which leads to a worse outcome (one prisoner's confession puts the other in jail, while both confessing puts them both in jail). Each prisoner's strategy will be influenced by many factors including the level of trust they have in the other person and their own perceived incentives for each course of action. But they would both be better off if they both stayed quiet and didn't implicate the other person.

There is a political prisoners' dilemma that results from the establishment cheating or changing the rules to benefit themselves. If the establishment doesn't cheat, and the outsiders don't accuse them of cheating, then both sides get a clean election. But if the establishment cheats, or the outsiders accuse the establishment of cheating, then they perceive themselves as better off. Ultimately this means the outsiders will accuse the establishment of cheating, and indeed the establishment will cheat, and therefore both sides- and the Party- are worse off and the prophecy is self-fulfilling.

21. Vice Presidential Selection

It is critical to remember that the presidential nominee does not select the vice presidential nominee. The national convention delegates choose the vice presidential nominee.

There aren't primaries for vice president, and therefore there is no binding of delegations. Delegates are free to vote their hearts and minds.

Therefore, it is highly possible - or even probable - that the losing side of the presidential contest makes a strong case for supporting a candidate for vice president against the wishes of the presidential nominee. For example, if an establishment candidate such as Jeb Bush, Marco Rubio, or John Kasich was to win the nomination for president, conservative outsider delegates may choose to support someone such as Ted Cruz or Ben Carson.

Usually the vice presidential selection is made with a rule in mind: Do no harm. Once that box is checked, one of the following strategies is usually used in the selection of a vice president.

1. *Consolidate a General Election* State - The media often builds its potential candidate lists based on the notion of a nominee using the vice presidential selection as a tactic to help win a state. With the possible exception of Clinton choosing Gore, this has actually occurred very seldom in modern times.

2. *Unify the Party* - Ronald Reagan was on the verge of selecting Gerald R. Ford as his running mate at the 1980 National Convention in Detroit until Ford went on TV and called the potential arrangement a co-presidency. At that point Reagan no longer wanted him as his running mate and instead chose former competitor George H.W. Bush despite the vitriol between the two campaigns. The decision was probably made as a way to quickly unite the party after the Ford decision was ruled out.

3. *Fix a Problem* - Barack Obama selected Joe Biden as his running mate probably to help alleviate concern over Obama's inexperience, specifically his lack of foreign policy expertise. Biden also offered appeal to the blue collar voters that Obama struggled with in Democrat primaries against Hillary Clinton.

4. *Double Down* - Bill Clinton from Arkansas chose Al Gore from Tennessee probably as a way to double down on the south and try to reverse or slow the trend of southern states moving towards the Republican nominee.

5. *Game Changer* - Occasionally there are races where a game changing selection is perceived to be required. John McCain was running against the first minority nominee of a major party and thought he needed a game changing selection as vice president. After initially preferring Democrat U.S. Senator Joe Lieberman in a unity ticket, he ended up choosing a female in Governor Sarah Palin.

A contested convention completely changes the dynamics involved in the vice presidential selection process. Every candidate with a real chance of becoming the nominee will name a vice presidential running mate as a tactic to try and win the convention. When the objective changes from being about winning the general election to about winning the convention, the strategy changes as well. The likely potential strategies at the Cleveland convention include:

1) *Consolidation* - Among the existing candidates, choose a running mate who has existing delegates. The most likely scenario is that existing candidates who won first ballot delegates in the nominating process team up into pairs of president and vice president. In some cases, this

might be to consolidate support on the ideological spectrum, in other cases to consolidate support on the outsider spectrum, or possibly make a cross-spectrum selection like Reagan did in 1976. Regardless it defines a strategy that brings two candidates together.

2) *State Delegation* – Choosing a candidate in order to win a particular delegation. This is a question of whether the candidates view the likelihood of a potential victory on the first ballot or on a later ballot. There is limited use to selecting a vice presidential nominee who does not have delegates allocated to them for the purpose of winning a state delegation because of the new rule mandating the binding of delegates on the first ballot. There will need to be a determination of what happens to bound delegates if their candidate drops out, suspends, or doesn't make the ballot. But assuming they can't vote for another candidate and are bound, then this strategy has limited potential on the first ballot. But it could have significant value on the second ballot by flipping a delegation that is now able to vote with their hearts and minds free from binding.

3) *Reshuffle* - There might always be a candidate who sees the necessity of trying to make a game changing selection as vice president to reshuffle the deck of cards. For example, maybe someone would select Sarah Palin again, or maybe Mitt Romney, or Paul Ryan, or someone else that would immediately grab the attention of the national convention delegates and scramble the math on the convention floor.

The problem is that this decision will be made with winning the convention in mind, rather than healing the party or winning the general election.

22. Established No Longer

There has been a longstanding riddle since the Tea Party movement first launched about what happens when the outsiders take over and the establishment no longer holds power.

The establishment is by definition the people who are in charge of the levers of power. So what happens when they are defeated? It happened at the RNC in 2009 when Michael Steele became Chairman and the establishment fought him tooth and nail, forming a shadow party until they were able to take power back from him by supporting one of his lieutenants.

We know the NRSC historically pulled support from Tea Party backed candidates, although they do a much better job under the new leadership of Ward Baker than they did previously.

But this riddle naturally leads to more questions than answers.

Would the establishment unite behind Donald Trump if he were to win enough delegates to become the presumptive nominee?

If not, would they unite behind him after he won the nomination with a majority of the delegates on the convention floor?

23. Total Chaos

The presidential nominating convention will be chaotic no matter how you look at it. The vast divide between the establishment and outsider wings of the party make it even more pronounced. Regardless of how well the Republican National Committee and Committee on Arrangements run the convention, it will be troublesome and problematic to deal with a contested convention atmosphere in a television and social media age.

Most likely, the noise will eventually settle and we will have a nominee after a couple of days of infighting. But it is always possible that total chaos ensues, and that the party is not capable of settling on a nominee or something else catastrophic occurs.

Here are some things that could lead to total chaos:

1) Ballot Access Controversies

Arguably the biggest disaster for the Republican National Committee would be if no candidate was able to achieve ballot access, and there wasn't a coalition on the Rules Committee or convention floor willing to change the rules.

But there are a number of other controversies that could happen relative to ballot access. What if one candidate was able to get support from a majority of eight delegations by winning delegations with few delegates or free agent delegations such as Guam, Virgin Islands, and American Samoa, but that candidate who achieved ballot access didn't have a majority of the delegates to the national convention? Or worse, what if another candidate had a majority, or at least a plurality?

The ballot access requirement has the potential to shift the national convention from chaos to total catastrophe.

2) Forced Vice Presidential Nominee

A contested convention means that there are a significant number of delegates who aren't supportive of the eventual nominee. As a result, it is highly possible that a disagreement ensues between the delegates and the nominee of the party over the selection of vice president.

There are a number of scenarios that could play out where the nominee's choice for vice president was not approved by the convention delegates. It could be for ideological reasons, outsider spectrum reasons, or simply that promises were made that can't be kept.

Probably the most likely scenario of a forced vice presidential nomination would be if a candidate won the nomination for president narrowly on the first ballot as a result of binding rules, but did not actually have the honest support of the delegates in their hearts and minds. This could lead the convention to express their displeasure by selecting a different nominee for vice president.

An alterative possibility would be for the losing presidential candidate in a multi-ballot convention could turn around and run for the vice presidential nomination and possibly win against the will of the nominee.

3) Rump Convention and/or Walkout

The convention usually will give the nominee of the party what he or she wants on most matters. But not always. The Dole campaign in 1996 wanted to contest California in the general election and eliminate the pro-life plank from the platform, and McCain preferred Joe Lieberman to be his running mate. But there were questions as to whether the convention would approve either of these things, and walkouts were a real possibility.

It is highly possible that the prisoners' dilemma of establishment cheating and accusations of cheating leads to significant dissension among delegates to the contention even after a nominee is selected. It isn't rare at hotly contested conventions for the losing side to accuse the winning side of cheating, walk out, and hold their own convention. It happened at the College Republican National Committee a few times over the years, and occurred on live TV at the 1988 Michigan State Convention.

What happens when a rump convention occurs at a Republican National Convention with thousands of reporters there to cover the chaos?

4) New Third Party

Any or all of these controversies could ultimately lead to the formation of a new third party similar to numerous other times in American history.

A candidate winning the nomination by default because of ballot access without having a true majority of the delegates could very well lead to a temporary third party. A controversy regarding the selection of the wrong vice presidential nominee could very well lead to a temporary third party. The establishment being accused of cheating and a walkout ensuing with a rump convention would almost certainly lead to a temporary third party.

The simple fact of an outsider winning the nomination might be enough for donors to form their own third party in the same manner they formed a shadow party when Michael Steele won the RNC Chairman position in 2009.

There will generally be plenty of potential for a third party to be formed by those who are disappointed with the results of the chaotic convention in Cleveland.

24. Cost of Chaos

There is a cost of chaos regardless of the outcome. It probably isn't a coincidence that brokered conventions stopped around the time that conventions started being televised. Voters tend to be turned off by infighting within a political party, and more importantly, it is relatively unattractive to see party bosses cutting deals and negotiating away the rights of voters to nominate a candidate.

Generally speaking, when there has been chaos at a national convention the candidate of that particular party loses. One can probably argue whether there is causation, and whether the chicken or the egg happened first, but regardless, there is a historical tendency for the chaotic convention to end in defeat.

The Republicans lost the last time their nominating convention went multiple ballots in 1948, and also lost in 1912 and 1940. The Democrats lost the last time theirs went multiple ballots in 1952, and also lost in 1920 and 1924.

The Republicans stopped having multi-ballot conventions after the Eisenhower vs. Taft convention in 1952. Although it was settled on the first ballot there were plenty of problems televised across the country. Republicans were able to win the presidency that year anyway, partially because Democrats had problems of their own at the 1952 Democratic Convention.

The other chaotic convention worth mentioning was the 1968 Democratic Convention in Chicago. The riots did nothing to help Democrats' chances of winning the White House.

So generally, a contested convention will create plenty of televised moments that will make swing voters cringe, but it won't make it impossible to win the general election.

The problems associated with voters watching conventioneering on TV are considerable. But even more damaging may be the potential for a high profile splitting of the party at the national convention that cannot be repaired in time.

An upset former candidate who refuses to support the nominee, can command a media microphone, and has enough support among the electorate to be considered somewhat credible would be catastrophic to Republican chances to win the White House.

Similarly, the contested convention in Cleveland risks that whichever side loses will walkout and ultimately choose not to support the winners, or even worse, create third party movement.

25. Potential Solutions

The easiest way to solve the chaos is by taking real steps to unite the party as part of the convention process. Here is what could be done:

1) Run a fair convention that does not bend the rules. There will likely end up being a working coalition that controls the Rules Committee and quite possibly clarifies, adjusts, or changes the rules. The people in power should not give in to the urge of the prisoner's dilemma and should value a fair convention process as helpful to winning the general election.

2) Candidates force their campaigns to reject the urge to blackball or otherwise mistreat activists, operatives, and donors who supported other candidates. Candidates should force their campaign teams to help heal the party.

3) The nominee should consider selecting the second place finisher as his or her vice presidential selection. This would be the easiest way to bring the party together and make sure a strong majority is working towards the ultimate goal of winning the White House. Or, congruently, the nominee should select someone from the opposite side of the outsider spectrum.

26. Conclusion

What do the 1860, 1948, and 1976 Republican National Conventions, the Howard Dean online campaign, the Obama 2008 campaign, and the rise of the Tea Party all have in common? Why should we care about them?

The 1860 Convention gave us Lincoln. The 1948 Convention gave us Truman and marked an important moment in defeating the southern bloc's power to stop the civil rights plank in the Democratic Party platform. 1976 gave us the launch of Ronald Reagan, and set him up as the frontrunner for 1980. In many ways, the Reagan Revolution was born at the 1976 Convention. Howard Dean's campaign proved that it was possible for a candidate who inspired the base of their party to circumvent the political establishment and raise enough money in small increments to compete and win. Four years later, Barack Obama cemented this theory, demolishing Hillary Clinton and shattering every known record for what a presidential candidate could raise.

Two years later on the GOP side, as a backlash against the Obama Stimulus and Obamacare, the Tea Party was born. Regular people, harnessing the power of information and technology stood up to the establishment of both parties and fought back. Across the country, candidates who in previous years never would have had a shot at victory were able to take on establishment frontrunners favored by the leadership of their party and win. Today, being the favored son of the establishment is no longer even a positive, it's negative if you are trying to win a primary.

The events described above are not just one off political events that are fun for historians to pick over. These are defining moments in the political history of our country that shaped so much of what came after, and yes, the way that we think about politics today and more importantly set us up for a chaotic national convention this summer. We are now engaged in one of the craziest, most interesting presidential primary seasons in American history.

As of this writing, we have a split decision between Iowa and New Hampshire. I am not going to predict winners and losers of future contests, but I will predict this: if we were going to have a contested convention in Cleveland, it would look exactly like what we see happening right now--no clear frontrunner, a split decision in the early states, outsider candidates buoyed by a base that is fed up with the establishment, candidates that can survive much longer than ever before because they have super PACs with tens of millions in the bank, a process that now means delegates are bound to vote for the candidate who won their state, and a number of rules questions that are uncertain at best. All of it points to the Republican Party heading into Cleveland unsure of who will emerge as the nominee and utter chaos for the national media to see.

Over the coming months, we are going to hear the media say over and over again, "This has never happened before!" In some ways, that will be true, as nothing ever happens the same exact way twice. But in other, important ways, we have historical guides to look at and guide us.

The Tea Party rise of 2010 is particularly important to understand as we think about this convention. It's almost impossible to overstate just how deep the antipathy is between the grassroots and the leadership of the Republican Party.

Go back to 2010: NRSC deliberately tried to kill Tea Party candidates in Senate primaries across the country. In 2012, the establishment got their preferred candidate in Mitt Romney and he was soundly defeated. The grassroots would argue that he was always a less than ideal candidate who ran a bad campaign with failed technology, the establishment would say that he was dragged too far right by conservatives in the primary process. Whomever you believe, there was plenty of finger pointing and acrimony after that defeat.

In 2014, Mitch McConnell promised to "repeal Obamacare root and branch" if Republicans were given control of the United States Senate. Republicans failed to stop the Iran Nuclear Deal, and did nothing to stop Obama's executive orders giving amnesty to illegal aliens. Note: There are good reasons for why Washington Republicans did what they did in each case, but that's not the point. The point is that the conservative base believes they were told in the 2014 campaign that if they gave Republicans control of the Senate, the Obama Agenda would be stopped. Rightly or wrongly, the base feels lied to.

Why does this matter? Because the anger at Republican leadership is so strong that it means that the establishment in Cleveland is going to be weaker than ever. Senators, congressmen, governors, all the folks who used to play such large, influential roles in conventions historically, will have less power, less influence, less ability to dictate to the delegates from their states than ever before.

Whatever the outcome, it's important for conservatives over the next few months to use history as a guide, to understand what is happening, to figure out the rules, and to be ready. We are either going to emerge from Cleveland stronger and more united than ever before, or a fractured shell of ourselves that leads to a third party.

These are fascinating, pivotal times that will define our politics for a generation. None of the outcomes are inevitable, but they are going to be critical in shaping the future of the GOP for generations.

See you in Cleveland.

About the Author

John Patrick Yob began his political involvement by attending Michigan State Conventions and Republican National Committee meetings with his father at a very young age, and serving as a page at the 1996 Republican National Convention in San Diego, CA.

He served as National General Chairman and Executive Director of the College Republican National Committee in 1999 after participating in College Republicans at the University of Michigan.

Today, Yob is known as one of the foremost Republican convention experts in the United States. He has run convention campaigns in roughly half the states across America. He has managed over fifty Michigan State Convention campaigns including multiple for Secretary of State, Attorney General, and Lt. Governor. He ran national convention operations for John McCain in 2008, Rick Santorum in 2012, and was National Political Director for Rand Paul in 2016.

Yob joined the John McCain operation as Great Lakes Political Director in 2005. He was elevated over the next few years to become National Political Director in 2007-8.

Yob was the lead Michigan Consultant for Rick Snyder's upset victory in the 2010 Governor's race and once again consulted for the 2014 General Election victory.

John built several successful companies over the last two decades at the intersection of campaigns and technology with the first emphasizing Computer and Technology Integration (CATI) in 2001. Additional companies handle general consulting, online consulting, online advertising, automated and live telephony, transaction processing, and merchant account banking.

John Yob and his wife Erica live at their home in St John USVI with their two children, Cassidy and Alexander.

Appendix A

Top Things You Can Do to Impact the Convention

1. Help your candidate win your state

There will be more states than ever before that are important to the selection process because if the nomination becomes a fight over a contested convention then every single state leading up to that convention will matter.

States like California, New Jersey, New York, Connecticut, and several others - that usually hold their primaries so late in the process that they don't matter - will now become critically important and possibly determinative in the nomination contest.

Simply put, every state and every vote matters for the first time in half a century. And winning a state matters even more than it did in previous cycles. Rules changes eliminated the dirty secret of beauty contests and mandated that the results of the primary or caucus are binding in most states (other than those who are free agents as a result of not having a presidential preference poll).

The binding of delegates means that on at least the first ballot the delegates will actually vote how they were supposed to have voted based on the result of the presidential preference vote in their respective state, and the corresponding national convention delegate allocation rules as submitted by the state GOP organization to the Republican National Committee.

So the most important thing you can do in the lead up to the convention is to help your candidate win your state. The more states your candidate wins, the better off he or she will be as the national convention approaches.

2. Participate in your state's national convention delegate selection process

You need to do more than just help your candidate win your state. The contested convention means that the names and faces that fill the delegate slots become absolutely critical to the campaigns - even those campaigns who lose your state.

For example, if your candidate loses your state, you will still want people elected to those delegate slots who will vote for convention committee members who will think for themselves and favor your candidate in tough committee votes. Just because Rubio wins your state doesn't mean the delegates from your state need to vote for committee members and in rules fights the way that the Rubio campaign tells them to. They are individual delegates who have the right to vote however they want on votes other than the actual nomination vote for president. They are not bound on rules votes, vice presidential votes, or any other vote aside from the presidential nomination vote.

Therefore, if your candidate loses your state, you want to support candidates for convention delegate who will think for themselves rather than blindly follow the candidate who won. In the extreme case, you could even support SINOs who pretend to support the candidate who won a particular delegate slot, but in reality will vote with another campaign on the key votes.

Alternatively, in the case that your preferred candidate wins your state, you must make certain that the people who are elected national convention delegate from your state actually support your candidate. There will certainly be people who pretend to support your candidate but are really SINOs who aren't being honest about their preferences and intentions.

3. Run for National Convention Delegate

The most important way to have a voice in a contested convention is to have a vote in a contested convention.

Immediately upon being elected delegate you will have the opportunity to elect a delegation chairman, and members of the various committees including the critical Rules Committee. The rules committee will give a report that recommends to the convention how ballot access will work, how binding will work, and other important decisions that can dramatically impact the ultimate selection of our nominees.

You will next have the opportunity to help your candidate get on the ballot by being one of the eight delegations that puts your candidate in nomination at the convention. It will be very difficult for any candidate to get a majority of eight delegations and therefore this could determine who wins the nomination regardless of who has the current lead in delegates.

Ultimately you will have a vote in the nomination of both president and vice president. It is very likely that the presidential nomination is hotly contested at the convention, and the result of that nomination contest could lead to a floor fight over the vice presidential nomination.

4. Persuade Free Agents

The most powerful positions at a Republican National Convention are delegates who are uncommitted or unbound and therefore can vote for whomever they want both for purposes of Republican National Convention ballot access and ultimately for the presidential nomination.

There are a very limited number of uncommitted delegates but there could be some elected in states and territories such as American Samoa, Virgin Islands, and Guam that have no preference vote and the delegates are unbound.

There are also likely to be some Uncommitted Delegates from Wyoming, Colorado, and North Dakota. The Super Delegates from states that do not hold a preference vote are also unbound.

5.   Persuade Super Delegates

The rule was changed prior to the 2008 national convention to make RNC Members Super Delegates to the Republican National Convention.

The three Republican National Committee members from every state, territory, and Washington, D.C. are Super Delegates to the Republican National Convention. This means that they are automatically given delegate slots and do not need to run for delegate in their respective state.

These people might be more sensitive to pressure from voters in their state because they have to run for re-election every four years in the case of RNC Members, and every two years in the case of the State Chairmen.

Most RNC Members are up for re-election at the time of the election of the national convention delegates and the State Chairmen will be up for re-election just six months after the Republican National Convention.

Therefore, they are interested in hearing from their constituents and you should let your voice be heard. If they ignore you, work against them in their races for party leadership and you will quickly earn their attention.

6.   *Run for State Chairman or RNC Member*

Many states have elections for Republican National Committeeman and Republican National Committeewoman at the same time, or similar time, that they have elections for National Convention delegate.

Members of the Republican National Committee serve "from convention to convention" - meaning those who are elected in the states officially hold the position at the gavel of the closing of the convention, and continue to hold the position until the gavel of the closing of the next convention.

Candidates for RNC Member who are elected in the states this year won't officially serve as RNC Member until the convention is over. However, members-elect are given better treatment at the convention and are informally recognized as leaders within their delegation.

There are also sometimes political benefits to being on a ticket with candidates for convention delegate so that the organization for your presidential candidate is stronger in your state in the lead up to the national convention.

You can announce that you, or a friend of yours, is going to challenge the sitting RNC member at the upcoming contest when national convention delegates are elected. The current RNC Member would still be a Super Delegate regardless of whether you were successful, but you can certainly get their attention by running against them. Most importantly, this will give you a vote in the election for RNC Chairman in January or February of 2017.

The election of a State Chairman is usually held after the November elections and it is often viewed as inappropriate to begin running for State Chairman before the general election is over. But you can start building a grassroots organization now that could be utilized to run for State Chairman later.

7. Organize Strategic Voting

The presidential campaign that wins a multi-ballot race at the Republican National Convention will probably be the campaign that does the best job of managing expectations and momentum from ballot to ballot.

As we previously demonstrated, in the multi-ballot races for RNC Chairman, it is critical to show an increase in support from ballot to ballot.

This is tricky given the binding rules that will limit how many state delegations can vote. But if you are a delegate to the national convention, or have friends who are delegates, then you could organize a strategic shift in voting to take place at a certain time.

It could take place among free agents while the binding rules are still in effect, it could take place on the first ballot that follows the lifting of binding rules, or it could take place on a ballot to be named later.

This could have an enormous impact on the momentum of the convention.

8. Organize Against a Bad Nominee

There are plenty of candidates in the race to like. There are plenty of candidates in the race to dislike. If you happen to have a candidate who you do not think would be a good candidate for President of the United States, then you could choose to work against that candidate as your top priority rather than working for any particular candidate as your top priority.

Some people just don't want Donald Trump to be President. Some don't want Marco Rubio to be President. Some don't want Ted Cruz to be President.

You can find like-minded people who are attending the convention as delegates, or who are friends with delegates, and convince them to team up to work against a particular candidate. This can be very powerful in a multi-candidate field.

The floor of the convention will be very unpredictable and there will need to be either temporary or permanent allies on the floor who don't necessarily support the same candidate for president.

The establishment and other groups of people will have tribes that they can work with. But who is your tribe? Build one and work against a bad nominee.

Made in the USA
San Bernardino, CA
23 February 2016